C000056276

LOUDER THAN WORDS

Catherine von Ruhland is a writer specializing in Green issues, and film. She is the author of *Going Green* (Marshall Pickering, 1991), *Glorious Food* (Marshall Pickering, 1992), and compiler of the anthology *Prayers from the Edge* (Triangle/SPCK, 1996). She lives in Teddington, Middlesex.

LOUDER THAN WORDS

An A–Z of Christian social action

CATHERINE VON RUHLAND

TRIANGLE

First published in Great Britain in 1997
Triangle
SPCK
Holy Trinity Church
Marylebone Road
London NW1 4DU

Copyright © 1997 Catherine von Ruhland

All rights reserved. No part of this book may be reproduced
or transmitted in any form or by any means, electronic or
mechanical, including photocopying, recording, or by any
information storage and retrieval system, without permission
in writing from the publisher.

While every possible care has been taken to ensure that
the statistics and facts given in this publication were accurate
at the time of publication, the publisher cannot accept
responsibility for incorrect information.

Bible references are taken from the
New International Version, © 1973, 1978, 1984

British Library Cataloguing in Publication Data

A catalogue record for this book is available from
the British Library.

ISBN 0–281–04931–9

Typeset by Pioneer Associates, Perthshire
Printed in Great Britain by
Caledonian International, Glasgow

CONTENTS

Introduction	1	ORGANIZATIONS	80
AIDS	3	POVERTY	84
BODY POLITICS	9	QUESTIONS	90
CHILDREN	14	RIGHTS	95
DISABILITY	20	SOCIETY	101
ENVIRONMENT	26	THIRD WORLD	105
FEMINISM	32	UNEMPLOYMENT	112
GAMBLING	38	VIDEO VIOLENCE	117
HOMELESSNESS	44	WAR	123
INVESTMENT	50	XENOPHOBIA	129
JUSTICE	56	YOUTH	135
KINGDOM	61	ZOOLOGY	141
LETTERS	66	*Notes*	148
MONEY	71	*Bibliography*	153
NEGATIVES	76	*Postscript*	169

For all who work in the Communications Department of Tear Fund, the Third World development agency; with thanks for their friendship, assistance and support during the compilation of Louder Than Words.

Then the King will say to those on his right, 'Come, you who are blessed by my Father; take your inheritance, the kingdom prepared for you since the creation of the world. For I was hungry and you gave me something to eat, I was thirsty and you gave me something to drink, I was a stranger and you invited me in, I needed clothes and you clothed me, I was sick and you looked after me, I was in prison and you came to visit me.'

Then the righteous will answer him, 'Lord, when did we see you hungry and feed you, or thirsty and give you something to drink? When did we see you a stranger and invite you in, or needing clothes and clothe you? When did we see you sick or in prison and go to visit you?'

The King will reply, 'I tell you the truth, whatever you did for one of the least of these brothers of mine, you did for me.'

Matthew 25.34–40

All that is necessary for the triumph of evil is that good people do nothing.

Edmund Burke

INTRODUCTION

Who we are as individuals is reflected in our actions. The condition of our heart, mind and soul is expressed in what we say and do, and how we respond to circumstances. As Christians, not only are we *called* to help others in God's name, but as our faith grows we find ourselves *desiring* to do his work too. His will becomes our own.

Therefore to interpret Christianity purely as a spiritual matter, without giving it any social role, is to limit God's purpose and to deny the power of love to change ourselves – and the effect we have on those we meet. 'As the body without the spirit is dead, so faith without deeds is dead,' wrote James.[1]

It is a truth that rings throughout Jesus' ministry on Earth. On one occasion, when a man asked him how a person could receive eternal life, Jesus turned the question back on the inquirer, saying, 'What do you think?' The man, a teacher of the law, knew his Scriptures: '"Love the Lord your God with all your heart and with all your soul and with all your strength and with all your mind"; and "Love your neighbour as yourself"'. That was correct. Jesus then told the story of the Good Samaritan: our neighbour was anyone in need, regardless of race or creed.[2]

Being both truly God and truly man, Jesus' life encapsulated the holism of spirit and flesh intended in our creation. His message – that to live fully one must love God, our neighbours and ourselves – was simple yet profound, and he healed people sick in body, mind and spirit. Ever conscious of his heavenly Father, he reached out and touched.

Two thousand years on, Jesus' lifestyle retains deep relevance for people's lives. Christians today have a responsibility to mirror his life of love in a time of great change and uncertainty. We don't have to make great gestures to make an impact, and it is often this misconception – and the fear it instils – that prevents us from offering our services at all. We fear that to get involved might demand more of our time and resources than we could possibly spare.

Louder Than Words takes heed of this tendency. Each chapter includes a ten-point plan of action, beginning with small steps that individuals can carry out, and culminating in great strides that could be undertaken by a local church. Within each chapter is a course of action that everyone can carry out. If readers find that they grow in concern for any particular issue, they can work their way through the point system and become more involved.

I do believe that it is time that Christians made an impact on the community at large. Politically, the UK – and Europe – is shifting to the 'Right'. In other words, the 'Left' is now on 'Centre' ground, leaving a wide-open gap for many of the nation's most needy people. The socially disadvantaged are becoming increasingly disenfranchised – and frustrated – as their voice is ignored. Scapegoats for society's ills are now identified in the form of single parents, travellers and the homeless. A quarter of the population, and one in three children, live in poverty, and the fact that many people are simply unaware of this – or choose to turn a blind eye – should disturb us. We have a duty to act now in love, to seek justice, speak the truth and make a practical difference, before we lose the chance.

I am thankful for the opportunity I have been given by my editor at Triangle, Naomi Starkey, to compile this book. I have learnt much in the course of its research and writing, and I pray that in some small way it will inspire others too.

CATHERINE VON RUHLAND

AIDS

'We're running scared. I cannot imagine a worse health problem this century.'
Dr Halfden Mahler of the World Health Organization

Facts of the matter

- The 1918–19 flu epidemic killed 26 million people world-wide. According to the World Health Organization estimates, by the year 2000, 30–40 million people will have contracted HIV, the virus that leads to AIDS.[1]
- In September 1994, the estimated number of cases of HIV infection was 500,000 in Western Europe, over 1 million in the USA, and 10 million in sub-Saharan Africa.
- Some 93 per cent of those with AIDS live in the Third World. Only 8 per cent of funding is directed to them.
- By 1998, 1 million Ugandans – 6 per cent of the population – will have died of AIDS.
- Half of all people with HIV are under 25. Most were infected in their teens.[2]
- AIDS is the leading cause of death among women aged 25–40 in New York City.[3]
- A total of 13,720 AIDS cases (around 10 men for every 1 woman infected) have been reported in the UK between 1982 (when reporting began) and the end of December 1996; 9,678 are known to have died. Over 60 per cent of infections were probably acquired through gay sex.[4]
- In the UK, 5 new cases of AIDS are diagnosed every day. Three-quarters of all known cases come from the Thames Health Regions.[5] In one London health authority district, AIDS is the leading cause of death among male residents aged 15–44.
- Some 11 per cent of UK AIDS cases, and 5 per cent of people with HIV, are aged over 50.[6]
- Approximately 1 in 200 of pregnant women anonymously

3

tested in inner London by antenatal clinics are HIV positive. Fewer than one-fifth of these women are aware of their status until the virus manifests itself in their new-born child.[7]

Introduction

In the early 1980s, a strange illness was reported to be spreading among the otherwise healthy young men of San Francisco's homosexual community. The condition – which struck at the victim's immune system, rendering him susceptible to other infections – was at first linked to the human body's apparent inability to withstand the frenetic, promiscuous living of many homosexual men.

Yet AIDS (Acquired Immune Deficiency Syndrome), as the 'gay cancer' later became known, spread by sexual intercourse, infected needles, and from mother to foetus, emerged in the USA and Africa at roughly the same time in the late Seventies. Africa had been slow to admit to AIDS since it feared damage to its tourism industry and cuts in foreign investment, but when sufferers began showing up among visitors and immigrants to Europe in 1981, scientists suspected a looming epidemic. In 1986, the then Health Minister Norman Fowler launched the British government's £28 million 'Don't Die Of Ignorance' campaign, and AIDS awareness became a top priority in the UK.

HIV, the virus that leads to AIDS, acts in a manner similar to flu. It has the ability to mutate into different sub-types, and so a vaccine that could destroy one strain could be useless against another. A cure, then, is remote, and the race is on between drug companies to find an effective treatment. While the transmission of AIDS is wholly preventable, the necessary change in behaviour that could wipe out the virus in a generation (that of remaining faithful to one, uninfected, sexual partner for life, and for drug addicts not to share needles), makes it extremely difficult – by the very nature of human behaviour – to contain the virus.

> 'The government got it wrong. There was no AIDS epidemic.'

In the UK, AIDS has yet to make a major impact on mainstream life, and more people will know somebody who has died of cancer or heart disease than from AIDS. But among homosexual men and drug addicts, AIDS has reached danger levels. For them, attending the funerals of friends is as frequent as for people in AIDS-stricken parts of Africa. While UK heterosexuals tend to turn a blind eye to what is happening *now*, the unnoticed HIV virus quietly and dangerously spreads.

> ## 'Isn't AIDS God's wrath on homosexuals?'

It has been pointed out that, in general terms, AIDS suits the views of the prejudiced. After all, they say, it affects drug addicts, gays and blacks. In reality, though, AIDS is transmitted via particular *behaviour* rather than simple *membership* of any particular group. In the West, AIDS has so far occurred largely among homosexual, intravenous drug user and bisexual communities. However, in the Third World, it has been predominantly through heterosexual intercourse, and in utero from the mother to her unborn child. Globally, 90 per cent of adult transmissions are a result of heterosexual transmission, and sexually active *homosexual women* are at least risk of all.

'There are many who believe this disease is God's vengeance, but I believe it was sent to teach people how to love and understand and have compassion for each other. I have learned more about love, selflessness, and human understanding in this great adventure in the world of AIDS than I ever did in the cut-throat, competitive world in which I spent my life.'

Psycho actor Anthony Perkins who died of AIDS, aged 60, in 1992.

> ## 'Good Christian people who never misbehave will not catch AIDS.'

After making this statement, the then Junior Health Minister Edwina Currie later claimed she was replying sarcastically to a letter in the press calling for the government to preach morality. As it happened, many were glad of the stand of her original statement, and many Jews disliked her implication that they led less than exemplary lives. Either way, what she said is not entirely true.

Many churches have members whose lifestyles changed

dramatically when they became Christians, but who may *already* have been infected with the HIV virus. Christian doctors and nurses are at risk from contact with infected blood in the course of their work. Additionally, not every Christian believes in remaining celibate until marriage. In many churches, homosexual and single heterosexual Christians are expected to remain chaste for life; but for many this can prove too tough a demand. Also, some faithful – and Christian – wives, and their children, are infected via a husband's adultery. In some African countries, girls are married younger as older, often infected, men exploit the girls' HIV-free status.

> 'Condoms? Or gloves to a burglar to protect him from broken glass?'

The emphasis on condom use to prevent AIDS concerns many Christians. Modern society's general flippancy towards the act of sex, ignoring the spiritual aspect of what it means to become 'one flesh' with another, goes against the grain for most believers.

Condoms make sex *safer* to the same extent that they act as contraceptives – that is, they do not provide 100 per cent certainty against conception *or* catching AIDS. Yet methods such as condoms, and needle exchanges for intravenous drug users, *do* save lives and – distributed with appropriate information – can help to change behaviour.

ACTION COUNTDOWN

'In response to the crisis of HIV and AIDS and its devastating effects on our communities, the challenge is for God's people to develop and demonstrate unconditional love in a compassionate, caring, healing and prophetic ministry.'

South African Council of Churches Mission Statement.

- **Become informed about AIDS**.
  To provide an effective response, it is vital to keep up to date with the facts.
- **Careless talk costs lives; stand up for the truth**.
  Be bold enough to speak out against dangerous ignorance, misinformation and homophobia.

- **Grieve with your gay friends for men who have died from AIDS.**
  Provide a shoulder to cry on. Attend a candlelit memorial service on World AIDS Day.
- **Donate money to support AIDS care**.
  Hospices and advice lines need urgent financial help if they are to continue their services.
- **Invite a speaker to your church, workplace or college**.
  AIDS organizations will provide a speaker, sometimes a person with AIDS, to talk about the issue.
- **Volunteer to do errands for a person with AIDS.**
  Your local council and AIDS groups will put you in touch with individuals who need help
- **Become a 'Buddy'.**
  Befriend an AIDS patient and help them to obtain care via the Terrence Higgins Trust (THT).
- **Start an AIDS awareness church group**.
  Meet for prayer, to share information and ideas for action, and as a local support group.
- **Adopt an AIDS orphan**.
  A growing number of children will lose parents as a result of AIDS, and may themselves be infected.
- **Set up an AIDS hospice**.
  Local churches can group together to set up much-needed community services and hospices.

MAKING CONTACT

ACET (AIDS Care, Education and Training), 27a Carlton Drive, LONDON SW15 2BQ. Tel: 0181 780 0400.

Catholic AIDS Link/Positively Catholic. Tel: 0171 485 7298.

Health Education Authority, Hamilton House, Mabledon Place, LONDON WC1H 9TX. Tel: 0171 383 3833.

London Lighthouse, 111–117 Lancaster Road, LONDON W11 1QT. Tel: 0171 792 1200.

Mildmay Mission Hospital, Hackney Road, LONDON E2 7NA. Tel: 0171 739 2331.

National AIDS Helpline. Tel: 0800 567123.

Public Health Laboratory Service Communicable Diseases Surveillance Centre, 61 Colindale Avenue, LONDON NW9 5EQ. Tel: 0181 200 6868.

Salvation Army AIDS Support Service, 105–109 Judd Street, LONDON WC1H 9TS. Tel: 0171 383 4230.

Terrence Higgins Trust (THT), 52–54 Grays Inn Road, LONDON WC1 8JU. Tel: 0171 831 0330.

(*THT Helpline*: Tel: 0171 242 1010.)

Almighty God, our heavenly Father who enabled your servant Job to go victoriously through great bodily suffering without denying your name, power and love, have mercy on us, Lord, who are stricken by this epidemic of AIDS.

Stretch out your healing hand and hold back this virus.

Strengthen and comfort in Jesus Christ those infected and ease their pain of body and mind.

Send your Holy Spirit to renew us all and lead us into repentance and faith in the gospel.

Give us the gift of discipline that we may keep our bodies and minds clean and holy.

Grant wisdom, knowledge and perseverance to all who seek a cure for AIDS that they may find the drugs to prevent and heal AIDS.

Have mercy on us, Lord, and all AIDS sufferers throughout the world.

Give love and compassion to all who seek to assist them through Jesus Christ our Lord,
Amen.

Prayer by Bishop Kauma of Uganda[8]

BODY POLITICS

'Therefore I tell you, do not worry about your life, what you will eat or drink; or about your body, what you will wear. Is not life more important than food, and the body more important than clothes? Look at the birds of the air; they do not sow or reap or store away in barns, and yet your heavenly Father feeds them. Are you not much more valuable than they?'

Jesus Christ

Introduction

Jesus' familiar words sound fine in principle, but it is difficult to trust him completely with our physical needs. How can we be sure that he will feed us if we are hard-up, when we know that every day across the world thousands of people, many fine Christians, die through lack of food or clean water? Or that he will clothe us when there are those with nothing more to wear than the rags in which they stand? And how can a God of love who resides in the spiritual realm provide the human, physical contact needed by somebody on their own?

There are no easy answers; even the incarnation does not provide them. A minister once wrote of offering solace to an inconsolable elderly lady afflicted by painful ill health. 'Jesus suffered too, you know,' he pointed out. 'Did he live to old age?' she spluttered, and continued with her weeping.

Yet even in the darkest moments when our physical needs seem to remain unmet, our only hope is to hang on to the remaining truth that God *is*. We are more than flesh and blood. There is a spiritual dimension to our existence that provides meaning to life. We must take care not to fall into the ancient heresy of separating flesh and spirit, because Jesus makes it clear that he has come to give us *full* life in body, mind and spirit. All are interconnected, and the fallen humanity that expresses itself via, say, pornography, eating disorders, ill health or abuse has a chance to get up off its knees, and be made whole.

> 'Pornography degrades women.'

Since 'beauty is in the eye of the beholder', those who publish or use pornography degrade themselves as much as those portrayed. Men's lifestyle magazines reveal what little respect their publishers have for their readership when they try to disguise 'soft porn' as fashion spreads.

Yet the Church must be careful how it expresses concern over such images. It is not enough to declare that pornography is offensive, for many people do not find it so. For the Church to align itself with a 1970s feminist stance is to miss the point that some pornography is now seen to give women power. These days, post-feminists argue that 'soft porn', which continues to present women in titillating, soft-focus shots and 'ripe for the taking', is far more exploitative than the *real* sex of 'hard porn', which presents women on an equal footing with men. (Many people believe that 'hard porn' is connected with sado-masochism, or similar things, but this is a complete misrepresentation of the differences between 'soft porn' and 'hard porn'.) However, the one point missing from the debate is what pornography, whether 'soft' or 'hard', does to the human spirit, dignity, sexuality and relationships of those involved – whether they like it or not.

> 'But "Page Three" is just a bit of harmless fun.'

When the MP Claire Short tried to ban 'Page Three' models from the nation's tabloid newspapers, she was ridiculed by a male press, yet received masses of mail from women who backed her. On view since 1975, the *Sun*'s 'Page Three' girl is a very British seaside postcard-style phenomenon, yet many women confronted every day in the workplace, and from their sons' bedroom walls, with this 'glamour' are left feeling very uncomfortable. Is this how men really view women? What is it saying to young girls about being a woman? And if women *are* taking it all a bit too seriously, why is it that so many men get uptight when the issue is broached?

> 'There are some things single Christians
> shouldn't know about.'

When tabloid newspapers and women's magazines use sex to sell copies, and most films of '12' certificate or over contain at least one gratuitous sex scene, to assume that unmarried Christians know nothing about sex – and that they somehow need to be protected – is extremely naïve. It is also incredibly patronizing. However, the parallel belief that 'you don't miss what you haven't had' – and that a quick hug during the Peace on a Sunday morning should satisfy the single person – is simplistic too. The Church must be sensitive to individuals trying to combine being a Christian and living alone. Many feel sad and neglected by God ('if the hairs on my head are counted, why doesn't he provide me with a partner to share my life?', they ask), and need genuine love, intimacy and understanding – and not platitudes.

> 'Since my body is the temple of the Holy Spirit, it
> ought to look good.'

What it means to 'look good' is largely culturally determined. In the West, it is 'good' to be slim, yet in more impoverished countries being overweight is regarded as a sign of beauty and status. Christians need therefore to be careful not to fall into the way of the world. To declare, for example, that fat people are simply greedy can reflect our media's obsession with presenting the ideal woman as 5'8" and a size 10. In reality, some 47 per cent of the UK's females – like Marilyn Monroe before them – are a size 16. It is important to keep fit, but God looks on the heart as much as the outer body. Whatever we look like, we should delight in our present beauty, knowing that we are fearfully and wonderfully made.

ACTION COUNTDOWN

'Even the hairs on your head are counted.'
Jesus Christ

- **Look in the mirror and tell yourself you're beautiful.**
  God says so! And self-esteem has a positive knock-on effect on those around you.

11

- **Look for the best in everyone**.
  If God thinks you're beautiful, he thinks everyone else is too. Therefore behold people with love.
- **Monitor how people are presented in the media.**
  Ask yourself what advertisements, news pictures and fashion shots say about men and women.
- **Ask your local newsagent and video store not to stock 'soft porn'.**
  Appeal to community spirit, and aim to raise the tone of things.
- **If you like what people wear and it suits them, tell them so**.
  Everyone likes a sincere compliment, even complete strangers!
- **Work on your mind, body and spirit on a daily basis.**
  Pray and read the Bible, walk the extra mile, or visit your local library.
- **Eat a balanced diet.**
  Improve your health chances by eating properly.
- **Rethink your wardrobe and dress with style for the creator God.**
  Shop at markets, army surplus stores and charity shops, or swap clothes with friends.
- **Set up a social group for local teenage girls – and another one for boys.**
  Help adolescents to discover the person God made them to be.
- **Set up a 'Healthy Living' group at your church.**
  Help people to consider the advantages and disadvantages of their way of life, and to improve their lifestyle.

MAKING CONTACT

Anorexia and Bulimia Care, 15 Fernhurst Gate, Aughton, ORMSKIRK, Lancashire L39 5ED. Tel: 01695 422479.

Anorexics Anonymous, 24 Westmoreland Road, LONDON SW13 9RY. Tel: 0181 878 9199.

Campaign Against Pornography, 9 Poland Street, LONDON W1V 3DE.

Care Trust, 53 Romney Street, LONDON SW1P 3RF. Tel: 0171 233 0455.

Christian Eating Disorder Centre, Higher Wembsworthy Farm, Hartland, BIDEFORD, North Devon EX39 6EN. Tel: 01237 441708.

Christian Eating Disorder Unit, 119 Wendover Road, AYLESBURY, Bucks HP21 9LW. Tel: 01296 330557.

Eating Disorders Association, Sackville Place, 44 Magdalene Street, NORWICH, Norfolk NR3 1JU. Tel: 01603 61909.

Henry Doubleday Research Association, Ryton Organic Gardens, Ryton-on-Dunsmore, COVENTRY CV8 3LG. Tel: 01203 303517.

Kairos Advisory Service for Eating Disorders, Flaxley House, Broadwater Road, HOLME-ON-SEA, nr Hunstanton, Norfolk PE36 6LQ.

National Viewers and Listeners Association, All Saints House, High Street, COLCHESTER, Essex CO1 1UG. Tel: 01206 561 155.

Soil Association, 86–88 Colston Street, BRISTOL BS1 5BB. Tel: 01179 290661.

Vegetarian Society, Parkdale, Dunham Road, ALTRINCHAM, Greater Manchester WA14 4QG. Tel: 0161 928 0793.

CHILDREN

'Vayishma Hashem et kol hayeled – "And God heard the cry of the child." Those words from Genesis 21 must never cease to echo in our minds. There is nothing more miraculous that we can be given than a child, and nothing more precious that we can give it than our love.'

The Chief Rabbi, Dr Jonathan Sacks

Facts of the matter

- One-third of the world's population is under 15, of whom 80 per cent live in the Third World.
- Some 75 per cent of all street children have some contact with their families; 5 per cent have no family at all.
- Up to 8 million children live on the streets of Brazil's cities.
- In Thailand, an estimated 500,000 girls under 18 (140,000 below 15), are prostitutes.[1]
- The International Labour Organization estimates that there are 100 million children under the age of 15 who are in employment, and 95 per cent of these live in the Third World.
- The average child in Europe receives £159 worth of toys each year (not including bicycles and computers), while American children receive £207 worth of toys.[2]
- In the UK, 1 in 4 households include a child under 16 years of age.
- Approximately 92 per cent of British children are state-educated.
- Some 30 per cent of UK inner-city children leave primary school 2 years behind in reading age.
- In Britain, 1 in 3 (4.2 million) children are living in poverty – compared with 1 in 10 in 1979. Some 70 per cent of these children live in families without a full-time worker.[3]
- The Children's Society reports 10-year-old girl prostitutes in Britain's cities.[4]

- Road accidents are the biggest single cause of death of under-18s in Britain.
- Over 1 million school-aged children in the UK have asthma.
- In 1995–96, the NSPCC's Child Protection Helpline received 67,431 calls.

Introduction

Children are our future, whatever their lifestyle, level of education, ability or race. Because they have little say in how their lives are run, how they are allowed to live says more about the adult world around them; and what they become echoes very much the treatment meted out to them when young. So often the abused becomes the abuser in later life; or, conversely, children who grow up under the wings of parents who clearly love each other, learn by example to love others and form deep relationships when it is their turn.

Modern Western culture puts particular strains on children. The Joseph Rowntree Foundation, the poverty research organization, has noted that in Britain two economically distinct types of parenting have emerged. Double-income families provide a high material standard of living, but the long hours worked by both parents mean that they spend little time with their children. Alternatively, lone parenthood, and the stresses and financial difficulties that go with it, have a knock-on effect on a child's well-being.

Childhood, as our own culture understands it, is a relatively new concept, evolving largely with the education system. Elsewhere, in the developing world, the role of the infant child – whose labour is vital to his or her family's survival – has changed little since biblical times, when Jesus brushed away the adults to focus his attention on those otherwise ignored.

> 'I blame it on the parents.'

As well as family environment, a child will be influenced by peer pressure, economic conditions, the mass media and the political culture in which he or she grows up. Everyone can help parents raise their offspring successfully by making sure that the optimum conditions prevail. Strong, healthy families are vital for a society's health. Devaluing society's basic unit can lead to a dangerous individualism that stresses little if any responsibility for others, especially the weak.

> 'I would never have been allowed to behave the way children do today.'

Older people have always looked upon the next generation with concern – and perhaps a little envy – regarding their behaviour. The generation gap is not so much about age difference, but the change in social mores since parents were children themselves. Where once children were 'seen and not heard' and never allowed to answer back, today there is a greater attempt to take account of their viewpoint. Certainly children can be brash and pushy – as can adults – but they gain confidence too as they sense their voice is being heard.

> 'A good bit of discipline never did me any harm.'

'Spare the rod and spoil the child' it used to be said, but fear instilled by too harsh discipline leads to cowed behaviour or, ultimately, deep rebellion. Of course, people need to know where the rails are in order not to go off them, but discipline must come in the context of a loving relationship with one's child. Children must be encouraged, rather than made to feel small, if they are to take a full and well-rounded role in society as future adults.

> 'My child needs a Christian education.'

Many Christians express concern that their local state school neglects teaching about Christianity in favour of a multi-faith approach. Many parents are worried by apparently poor standards of education at state schools, though they fail to consider whether the same might be true of private schools. Labour MP Harriet Harman caused wrath on both sides of the House of Commons when she, like her party leader before her, sent her son to a grant-maintained school, whilst the then Shadow Education Secretary David Blunkett was adamant that selective education was not the Labour Party's policy. By their actions, Harriet Harman and Tony Blair were declaring that the schooling they would choose for other people's' children was not good enough for their own.

If people believe in the importance of a good education for *all* children regardless of a parent's income or where they happen to live, then middle-class professionals, Christians among them, would do well to support their local school. Intelligent, articulate, educated members of society have a strong capacity to promote change and improvements where there is need. Rather than opting out of a system with which one might be unhappy, it is arguably more Christian to make a stand on behalf of others less able or fortunate.

> 'Haven't they got anything better to do than hang around the streets?'

Profound poverty and family breakdown have caused the number of street children world-wide to soar. Millions of rural families have migrated to the slums of the world's cities in search of a better life, but, with little work available and no social security, children must also work to help the family survive – often risking their lives daily. In the UK, neglected youths from local authority homes, many hooked on drugs, are known to prostitute themselves in the red light districts of the nation's major cities. Adults must provide an adequate social support system so that these young people can receive the care they need.

ACTION COUNTDOWN

'Whoever welcomes a little child like this in my name welcomes me. But if anyone causes one of these little ones who believe in me to sin, it would be better for him to have a large millstone hung around his neck and to be drowned in the depths of the sea.'

Jesus Christ

- **Take account of children.**
  Aim to see things from their point of view. Listen to what they have to say. Give them time.

- **Avoid buying products made by companies that use child labour.**
  Some 11 per cent of the workforce in some Asian countries are children. Contact the World Development Movement (see the Making Contact section) for details.
- **Avoid pressures to supply your child with the latest consumer trend.**
  Use toy libraries and parks so that they learn to share and meet and play with others.
- **Write to your MP**.
  Ensure your MP is a Parliamentary Friend of the NSPCC so that children's concerns are debated.
- **Contact the NSPCC on how to promote its free Child Protection Line.**
  Enable people worried about children at risk, and the children themselves, to turn to the right support agencies for help.
- **Volunteer to be a Sunday School teacher.**
  Also, consider the possibility of training in childcare or teaching.
- **Start up a weekday children's group at your church.**
  With limited nursery places, many pre-school children lose out on social interaction.
- **Provide a child drop-off centre at your church hall during shop opening hours.**
  Work with local traders, businesses, the council and the NSPCC to set up a scheme.
- **Set up an After-School Centre.**
  If both parents work, often there is no one at home when children finish school.
- **Sponsor, foster or adopt a child or teenager.**
  Provide a loving place of refuge, or make a commitment to sponsor a Third World child by making regular payments via a relevant charity.

MAKING CONTACT

Action Aid, Hamlyn House, MacDonald Road, Archway, LONDON N19 5PG. Tel: 0171 281 4101.

British Agencies for Adoption and Fostering, Skyline House, 200 Union Street, LONDON SE1 0LX. Tel: 0171 593 2000.

Child Poverty Action Group, 1–5 Bath Street, LONDON
EC1V 9PY. Tel: 0171 253 3406.

The Children's Society, Edward Rudolf House,
69–85 Margery Street, LONDON WC1X OJL. Tel: 0171 837 4299.

Exploring Parenthood, 4 Ivory Place, Treadgold Street,
LONDON W11 4BP. Tel: 0171 221 4471.

Jubilee Action, St John's, Cranleigh Road, Wonersh, GUILDFORD,
Surrey GU5 0QX. Tel: 01483 894787. (Charitable, fund-raising
work.)

Jubilee Campaign. (Political, non-charitable work): see Jubilee
Action.

National Children's Bureau, 8 Wakley Street, LONDON
EC1V 7QE. Tel: 0171 843 6000.

NSPCC, 42 Curtain Road, LONDON EC2A 3NH. Tel: 0171 825 2500.

NSPCC Child Protection Helpline. 24 hour free service:
Tel: 0800 800 500.

Save the Children, 17 Grove Lane, Camberwell. LONDON
SE5 8RD. Tel: 0171 703 5400.

Scripture Union, 207–209 Queensway, Bletchley, MILTON KEYNES,
Buckinghamshire MK2 2EB. Tel: 01908 856000.

Tear Fund, 100 Church Road, TEDDINGTON, Middlesex
TW11 8QE. Tel: 0181 977 9144.

UNICEF, 55 Lincoln's Inn Fields, LONDON WC2A 3NB.
Tel: 0171 405 5592.

World Development Movement (WDM), 25 Beehive Place,
LONDON SW9 7QR. Tel: 0171 737 6215

World Vision UK, 599 Avebury Boulevard, MILTON KEYNES,
Buckinghamshire MK9 3PG. Tel: 01908 841000.

Y Care International, 640 Forest Road, LONDON E17 3DZ.
Tel: 0181 520 5599.

DISABILITY

'Your faith has made you well.'
Jesus Christ

Facts of the matter

- In Britain, 1 in 3 people will contract cancer, of whom around 50 per cent will die within 5 years.[1]
- Breast cancer is the main cause of death in women aged 35–55 in Britain. In any one year, 25,000 women will learn they have breast cancer; 1 in 12 women in the UK will develop this disease at some point in their lives. Some 15,000 women die from the disease each year.[2]
- Of 300,000 women aged 85 or over who are ill, 200,000 of them live alone.[3]
- Arthritis affects 1 in 10 people in the UK, and is one of the biggest problems of ageing.[4]
- Annually, around 100,000 people die from smoking-related illnesses in the UK.
- According to government statistics, 1 in 10 people and 1 in 5 children suffer mental illness severe enough to need professional assistance.
- Some 5,000 kidney patients are presently on 'death row', dependent on dialysis machines while they await kidney transplants. Approximately 2,000 of these people will receive transplants this year, the remainder to be joined in the queue by the thousands more who are experiencing kidney failure.
- According to the Department of Social Security, 1 in 30 people of working age have been off work for over a year as a result of sickness or accident.
- Some 39 million Americans – 1 in 7 of the population – have no health insurance.[5]

Introduction

No one is born perfect, and no one can ensure total immunity from one medical condition or other at some point in their life. Genetically, there is some biological defect, however minor, in each of our families. It could range from shortsightedness, high blood pressure, diabetes to heart disease. As we get older, the natural process of ageing will diminish our physical and mental capabilities. It is therefore misguided to assume that 'the disabled' are other people. There will always be sick and vulnerable people who need help in carrying out everyday tasks, and it is surely Christian to do so. At the very least, to ensure that disabled people have adequate services is an investment for our own and our families' futures!

Jesus said that the poor will always be with us; and there will always be a percentage of any community handicapped by their physical or mental condition. How a society regards and treats its most disabled, most vulnerable citizens reveals something about its basic values. While it is difficult to provide for every eventuality, in developed countries provision of wheelchair ramps, hearing aid loops and large-print signs in public places should be standard to ensure that as many people as possible can lead independent lives – and contribute something to the society in which they live.

> 'I don't have to worry, I've made sure
> I'm insured.'

Individuals with spare money can choose to insure against falling ill or having an accident, yet it is the healthier members of the population who benefit, for those most in need of medical care – diabetics, people with AIDS, handicapped children, anyone with an *already diagnosed* condition – cannot receive cover for it. The people most dependent on life-long medical treatment are denied anything but that which the increasingly undervalued, undermined National Health Service can offer. Already, where once long-stay patients could remain in hospital, they are now returned to the community and the responsibility of various social services. Many, often elderly, people still in need of convalescence must fend for themselves, or rely on the goodwill of friends and family. Those who have saved money throughout their lives are seeing it dwindle on care that they had at the time rightfully assumed would be provided by the State.

> 'Disabled people are here to draw the best
> out of their carers.'

Families, friends and carers of disabled people can find hidden strengths as a result of their relationships with them, but it is utilitarian to regard an individual's *raison d'être* as purely for the benefit of others. Disabled people are individuals in their own right, and so deserve basic respect. They have talents they can contribute to society, and negative traits too. They are of value because they are human beings made in God's image. Nothing more; nothing less.

> 'Why should we provide facilities for disabled
> people anyway?'

The severely disabled Stephen Hawking, David Blunkett and Jack Ashley, and the late Jacqueline du Pré, Dennis Potter, and Paul Eddington, have all richly contributed to recent British culture. Wheelchair, voice box, guide dog, hearing aid and skin treatments helped them reach their full potential.

The Care in the Community scheme revealed the sheer danger of releasing mentally ill people from long-stay hospitals on to the streets without adequate follow-up. Adults with a long-term illness must now prove to an independent tribunal, not their GP, that they need Incapacity Benefit. Those with difficult to determine conditions, such as ME (often known as Chronic Fatigue Syndrome) or RSI (Repetitive Strain Injury), are falling through the social security net. The growing elderly population puts pressure on medical and social welfare systems. Survivors of once fatal illnesses, such as strokes and heart disease, often remain seriously handicapped. It is vital that disabled people of any age receive help.

> 'Is organ donorship really Christian?'

Although 80 per cent of British people are in favour of donating their organs (but only 30 per cent carry a card), many Christians, perhaps mindful of Levitican laws regarding the spilling of blood, remain unsure about the ethics of sharing their body parts. Is it not 'unnatural' for an individual to be reliant on another's vital organs to stay alive? Is it somehow disruptive of God's plan of action to prolong somebody's life in this way? And where does one person begin and another end? Yet those who have literally been given a new lease of life are thankful for their second chance, and a growing number of Christians, who would not be alive today but for such medical practice, have an extra opportunity to serve God on this earth.

'We didn't need counselling in my day.'

A shoulder to cry on and a listening ear are always of value. Shell-shocked First World War veterans clearly needed psychological treatment, and sexually abused Viennese women sought help from Sigmund Freud (though he ultimately betrayed them, explaining away their experiences as unconscious desires). Prayer and confession is arguably as much a psychological help as a spiritual one. Presenting the stoical British 'stiff upper lip' in the face of deep hurt ironically bottles up problems for the future and future generations, preventing a break with the past.

The provision of counsellors for adolescents grieving over the split-up of the pop group Take That (and similar instances of counselling being offered for seemingly trivial events) has devalued counselling in the eyes of many people. However, being helped by a trained, sensitive counsellor in the wake of *real* tragedy has been of enormous benefit to some people, enabling them to work their way through their grief to a more positive future.

ACTION COUNTDOWN

The King will reply, "I tell you the truth, whatever you did for one of the least of these brothers of mine, you did for me." '

Jesus Christ

- **Read A. J Cronin's *The Citadel*, a book about a young pre-NHS doctor**.
  Also, ask older friends and relatives what life was like before the National Health Service.

- **Write to your MP.**
  The issue of dwindling NHS dentists is foremost in some MPs' mail. Free NHS glasses are no longer available; people on income support receive a paltry £26.50 voucher towards the cost of spectacles.
- **Open your eyes to the daily difficulties faced by disabled people.**
  Campaign for better access and facilities on public transport systems and in buildings.
- **Focus on a particular disability – use the Making Contact section for guidance.**
  Become informed, campaign, and raise money on behalf of people with a specific disability.
- **Register as an organ donor, and let your family know of your wishes.**
  Your two kidneys alone could transform four lives; call 0990 600699 to register.
- **Give blood.**
  Help others live; ring 0345 711 711 for details of your nearest Donor Centre.
- **Learn First Aid by training with the Red Cross or St John's Ambulance.**
  Or join the Casualties Union to help train professional medics.
- **Learn sign language to communicate with people who are deaf.**
  Check with local colleges for evening classes.
- **Befriend an elderly, disabled or sick person, and visit them regularly.**
  Learn from the example of AIDS charities, and set up a care system in your community.
- **Train to be a carer.**
  Qualify as a doctor, nurse, counsellor, hospital or home help; use your skills to serve others.

MAKING CONTACT

Age Concern, Astral House, 1268 London Road, LONDON SW16 4ER. Tel: 0181 679 8000.

Breast Cancer Campaign, 15–19 Britten Street, LONDON SW3 3TZ. Tel: 0171 867 1103. (*Nationwide Freeline*: Tel: 0500 245 345.)

Cancer Information Service: 0171 613 2121.

Casualties Union, PO Box 707A Friend Street, LONDON EC1V 7NE. Tel: 0171 278 6264.

Cerebral Palsy Helpline: 0800 626216.

Department of Health, Skipton House, 80 London Road, LONDON SE1 6LW. Tel: 0171 972 2000.

Doctors and Lawyers for Responsible Medicine, 104b Weston Park, LONDON N8 9PP. Tel: 0181 340 9813.

Healthcare Christian Fellowship, 349 Beersbridge Road, BELFAST BT5 5DS.

Mencap, 123 Golden Lane, LONDON EC1Y ORT. Tel: 0171 454 0454.

Multiple Sclerosis Society, 25 Effie Road, Fulham, LONDON SW6 1EE. Tel: 0171 736 6267. (*Helpline*: Tel: 0171 371 8000.) *Scottish Office*: 2A North Charlotte Street, EDINBURGH EH2 4HR. Tel: 0131 225 3600. *Northern Ireland Office*: 34 Annadale Avenue, BELFAST BT7 3JJ. Tel: 01232 644914.

RAD (Royal Association in aid of Deaf People), 27 Old Oak Road, Acton, LONDON W3 7HN. Tel: 0181 743 6187

RNIB (Royal National Institute for the Blind), 224 Great Portland Street, LONDON W1N 6AA. Tel: 0171 388 1266.

RNID (Royal National Institute for Deaf People), 19–23 Featherstone Street, LONDON EC1Y 8SL. Tel: 0171 296 8000.

Scope (previously The Spastics Society), 12 Park Crescent, LONDON W1N 4EQ. Tel: 0171 636 5020.

Women's Health Concern, 93 Upper Richmond Road, LONDON SW15. Tel: 0181 780 3916. (*Helpline*: 0181 780 3007.)

ENVIRONMENT

'Only when the last tree has died and the last river been poisoned and the last fish been caught will we realize we cannot eat money.'

Native American saying

Facts of the matter

- Out of the warmest years on record, 9 out of 10 have occurred since the early 1980s.
- There are 7,500 manmade objects currently being tracked in the Earth's orbit. Only 5 per cent of them are operational spacecraft.[1]
- Approximately 50 million acres of tropical forest and 24 billion tonnes of soil are lost annually. Some 43 per cent of the world's forest cover has already disappeared, most of it during the 1980s. The World Wide Fund for Nature claims that 25 per cent of known medicines come from rainforests.
- Each year, 93 million extra people need 28 million more tons of grain to feed them.[2]
- US companies earn $500 million a year from world sales of US-banned pesticides.[3]
- Some 9 million people have been affected by the 1986 Chernobyl nuclear power plant disaster.
- Road transport is the single biggest cause of air pollution in the UK, accounting for 99 per cent of London's carbon dioxide emissions, and 14 per cent of UK pollution as a whole. There are 21 million cars on the roads in the UK.[4]
- The National Trust is the largest private landowner in Britain, protecting over 238,000 acres of countryside and more than 550 miles of coastline.
- All local authorities now have a government directive to recycle 25 per cent of household waste by the year 2000.
- Over 200 Sites of Special Scientific Interest are damaged or destroyed annually.[5]

- Every year, 4,000 miles of English hedgerow, plus wildlife and flowers, are lost.[6]

Introduction

We all make a deep imprint on the local, national and global environment via the lives we lead. However much we as individuals or nations aim to stem the flow of bad practice, our previous actions have consequences. The human race has left traces in the marine sediment in the depths of the seas, in the snow of the world's highest mountain tops, and beyond into the sky and outer space.

There has been periodic concern for the environment. The 'small is beautiful' *conservationism* of the late 1960s and early 1970s gave way in the mid-1980s to a massive public surge of Green *consumerism*. However, many Christians had to be convinced that environmentalism wasn't some New Age fad, missing the point that they should *always* have been concerned about God's creation, and that part of our worship is about reclaiming this sinful Earth for his glory.

To take such a Christian lifestyle seriously will soon lead us to recognize that the political and economic assumptions and systems under which we presently live contradict our position of faith. A system that worships economic *growth* above all else (whether the system comes from the Left or Right) is not only *spiritually* futile, but a threat to the very existence of planet Earth and all creatures who live here. The world is a finite place that cannot, and should not, be plundered as if there were no tomorrow. For example, the amount of water that exists (regardless of its form) remains constant, so while heavy seas may appear to disperse oil spills easily, the oil has not diminished in *quantity*, and therefore the water is no less polluted. The world's ecosystems are finely balanced webs of existence, and damage or loss of one small strand reverberates globally, and we are the poorer for it.

> 'Caring about the environment is a luxury.'

A recession concentrates people's minds on short-term commercial success – and it is easy to lose any Green vision we might

27

have had. Certainly for those on low incomes, being a Green consumer can seem financially out of reach. Many 'environmentally friendly' brands on our supermarket shelves are notably more expensive than ordinary, not so Green, products. In the developing world, the environmental impact of the poor is more obvious. Rainforest is replaced with pasture land for beef cattle, and the burning timber contributes to the 'greenhouse effect'. The poor then have to go deeper into the jungles to find suitable land.

However, the make-do-and-mend mentality that enabled British families to get through the war and post-war years – and that was integral to the early 1970s period of environmentalism – stands people in good stead when they have a low income. By repairing broken furniture, making and altering clothes to suit current trends, growing fruit and vegetables, and being an inventive cook, we become more aware of the sheer waste of our shopping culture.

Such practices lie at the base of many less economically developed cultures than our own. Those who work on the land or fish the seas know that their harvesting must be sustainable, and that to over-indulge, as is the message of our own culture, is ultimately shortsighted and self-destructive. Our Western way of life is a luxury that planet Earth cannot afford.

> 'The human race is ingenious. We'll replace whatever runs out.'

The developed world's incessant pursuit of economic and technological progress at all cost gives us little time to wonder at its value. We have lost the wisdom of our forebears. Instead of caring for what has been left to us, so that we hand it on in good condition to those who follow us, we have chosen to plunder and consume.

'Our present situation of rapid material growth, which encourages every family to expect as of right an ever-expanding surplus, is, in the light of man's long history, so abnormal that one knows it has to cease. Sooner or later the curves have to flatten out. And if the quality of our children's life in this world

*is of any concern of ours, then, in the industrialized countries
at least, the sooner the better.'*

Michael Taylor of Christian Aid

'With the full-blown greenhouse effect, we
won't need foreign holidays.'

The 1980s were the hottest decade on record, and in September
1995 a record ozone hole the size of Europe formed over
Antarctica – hardening the mood of naïve optimism among many
people that summer in Britain might soon be worth staying
around for. It is a frightening and rather sick and selfish assump-
tion that chooses to ignore the disruption from major atmospheric
changes to the entire planetary ecosystem, and the health of its
inhabitants, as regions experience freak weather conditions. Mass
migration of people and animals will follow the inevitable deaths
of so many others, so it is not something to which we should be
looking forward. Our role is to keep abreast of scientific findings
on climate change, and aim in our lives to reduce the pressure
on the Earth and its atmosphere.

ACTION COUNTDOWN

*'God means his world to be managed by Man, not exploited, and
Christians ought to be among the first to raise their voices
against all that would destroy rather than preserve the richness
and the beauty of God's world – our home.'*

The Right Reverend Robert Williamson, Bishop of Bradford

- **'Be still and know that I am God.'**
  Be quiet in order to hear the sound of God's creation: birds, chil-
  dren playing, the wind in the trees . . .
- **Undertake a personal audit.**
  'Think of a personal place from childhood – a beach, perhaps,
  or a wood, or a street corner. Is it the same? Is it cleaner, qui-
  eter, less crowded? Is it *there*?'[7]
- **Plant a tree.**
  Nurture seedlings and plant them in spaces where they have a
  chance to grow.

- **Dig a pond for your back garden.**
  Encourage frogs, newts and pond insects back into your community.
- **Attend a church within walking distance.**
  Every church is a community church; find one to suit you within a mile of your home.
- **Use public transport.**
  As Sir David Attenborough says, 'You don't need a car if you live in London.' Or use a bicycle.
- **Convert your church grounds into a nature reserve.**
  If churchgoers *did* leave their cars at home, there'd be more space for wildlife to flourish.
- **Make a point of using your local shops and services.**
  Support your community, and cut down on transport pollution and over-packaging.
- **Refrain from eating at fast-food restaurants.**
  Avoid the creeping Americanization, junk food and junk values of 'Burger Bars'.
- **Aim for zero population growth: one birth per parent.**
  Consider adoption or fostering instead of having more children.

MAKING CONTACT

British Trust for Conservation Volunteers (BTCV),
36 St Mary's Street, WALLINGFORD, Oxfordshire OX10 OEU. Tel: 01491 839766.

Centre for Alternative Technology (CAT), Llwyngwem Quarry, MACHYNLLETH, Powys, Wales SY20 9AZ. Tel: 01654 702400.

Christian Ecology Link, 20 Carlton Road, HARROGATE, North Yorkshire HG2 8DD. Tel: 01423 871616.

Commonwealth Human Ecology Council (CHEC), 57/58 Stanhope Gardens, LONDON SW7 5RF. Tel: 0171 373 6761.

Council for the Preservation of Rural England (CPRE), Warwick House, 25 Buckingham Palace Road, LONDON SW1W OPP. Tel: 0171 976 6433.

Earthscan, 120 Pentonville Road, LONDON N1 9JN. Tel: 0171 278 0433.

Earthwatch Europe, 57 Woodstock Road, OXFORD OX2 6HJ. Tel: 01865 311600.

Environment Agency, Rio House, Waterside Drive, Aztec West, Almondsbury, BRISTOL BS12 4UD. Tel: 01454 624 400.

Environmental Investigation Agency, 15 Bowling Green Lane, LONDON EC1R 1BD. Tel: 0171 490 7040.

Friends of the Earth (FoE), 26–28 Underwood Street, LONDON N1 7JQ. Tel: 0171 490 1555.

Friends of the Earth (FoE) Scotland, Bonnington Mill, 70–72 New Haven Road, EDINBURGH EH6 5QG. Tel: 0131 554 9977.

Greenpeace, Greenpeace House, Canonbury Villas, LONDON N1 2PN. Tel: 0171 865 8100.

Henry Doubleday Research Association:
see **B – BODY POLITICS**

Railway Development Society, Little Close, 13 Arnhill Road, Gretton, CORBY, Northamptonshire NN17 3DN.

Ramblers Association (RA), 1–5 Wandsworth Road, LONDON SW8 2XX. Tel: 0171 582 6878.

Religious Education and Environment Programme (REEP), 8th Floor, Rodwell House, Middlesex Street, LONDON E1 7HJ. Tel: 0171 377 0604.

Royal Society for the Protection of Birds (RSPB), The Lodge, Sandy, Bedfordshire SG19 2DL. Tel: 01767 680551.

Transport 2000, Walkden House, 10 Melton Street, LONDON NW1 2EJ. Tel: 0171 388 8386.

Wildlife Trusts (Royal Society for Nature Conservation), The Green, Wiltham Park, Waterside South, LINCOLN LN5 7JR. Tel: 01522 544400.

Women's Environmental Network (WEN), 87 Worship Street, LONDON EC2. Tel: 0171 247 3327.

WWF (UK) (World Wide Fund for Nature), Panda House, Weyside Park, GODALMING, Surrey GU7 1XR. Tel: 01483 426444.

FEMINISM

'Women are half the world's population, one third of the official workforce, and do two thirds of the world's work-hours. Yet they receive only one-tenth of the world's income and own less than one-hundredth of the world's property.'

United Nations

Facts of the matter

- If girls were valued as boys are, 100 million more women would exist world-wide. (In the Third World, male offspring are better fed, receive superior healthcare, etc. These factors operate alongside the policy of abortions of female foetuses.)[1]
- Some 500,000 women die each year during childbirth or while they are pregnant. A quarter of these women are teenagers. For every woman who dies, a hundred others are left sick or disabled. UNICEF claims that 100,000 deaths occur annually as a result of unsafe abortions.
- In Bombay, of 8,000 foetuses aborted once parents knew its sex, only 1 was a boy.[2]
- Some 45 per cent of the world's women are illiterate.
- World-wide, women receive an average 35 per cent less pay than men for the same work.
- Only 33 per cent of the Third World's women are in paid employment.
- Only 6 countries in the world have women leaders.
- Every 6 minutes, a rape is reported in the USA. Some 25 per cent are by 2 or more assailants.[3]
- Only 63 out of 651 British MPs are female.
- Out of 300 detective inspectors in the Metropolitan Police Service, only 10 are women.[4]
- About 22 per cent of UK administrators/managers, and 39 per cent of technicians/professionals, are women.
- Despite 20 years of equal pay legislation, women's gross

hourly earnings in Britain are only 79 per cent of men's. British women have the second lowest wages in Europe.

- Approximately 60 per cent of Britain's informal carers for the sick and elderly are female.
- Some 90 per cent of Britain's lone parents are women.[5]
- In a study of 1,000 adults in Islington, London, two-thirds of men admitted they would use violence on their partners in 'conflict' situations. Of 1,000 young people in Edinburgh, two-thirds of boys believed they would probably use violence in future relationships.[6]

Introduction

'Feminism' is a dirty word to some, but the influence of the women's movement throughout this century has been vital, though the struggle for women's equality continues. Before women in the UK got the vote, even the brightest woman was in effect regarded as incapable of political thought. Today, girls consistently outperform boys in GCSEs. Women still find it difficult to break through the 'glass ceiling' above which men run the 'corridors of power', yet more than ever they are committed to achieving their full career potential. Therefore they are very frustrated when their ambitions are unrealized purely on the grounds of their sex. Never before in the history of the Church have there been so many graduate Christian women, yet the positive contribution they could make to the Church and society remains undervalued.

Pregnancy and childcare are the main reasons why women give up their careers, therefore many have children at a later age or have none at all. It is predicted that 1 in 5 of UK women presently below the age of 40 will never have children. Today's women, products of the groundbreaking 1960s women's movement, expect more from their partners than their mothers anticipated from theirs.

Elsewhere, females face far less subtle discrimination than in the West. In a culture where having boys is a sign of status, female foetuses will be aborted, as in India. When your government decrees a 'one child per family' policy to control population, girls will be dumped in 'orphanages' to die unattended, as in China. In Africa, women are homeworkers *and* responsible for over 60 per cent of agricultural work. Without their labour, the African continent would grind to a standstill, yet the United Nations estimates that only 5 per cent of aid is targeted directly at women.

Women's rights is not a fringe issue; it is one of justice directly affecting half the world's population – plus their families. It is a question of human rights.

> 'Investing in men makes far more
> economic sense.'

Across the world, girls receive less education, less food and less healthcare than boys. Yet what happens to females has a profound impact on the well-being of entire countries; children's health and mortality rates are affected much more by a mother's schooling than by their father's. Educated women are less at risk of dangerous pregnancy, for they are more likely to delay marrying, have fewer children, and seek healthcare before and after pregnancy.

Most government and international statistics devalue women's work because much is unpaid and so, in economic terms, invisible. While in the Third World it is women who are the water carriers from a young age, it is the decision-making men of the community who discuss the improvement of water supply systems and keeping water clean. Since 80 per cent of the world's diseases could be eradicated with clean water, improved sanitation, better nutrition and preventative healthcare, it is vital that health projects include and train women.

> 'Women aren't capable of doing the same
> jobs as men.'

In the Third World, it is obvious that this is not so. In Lesotho, 90 per cent of the roads were built by women. In the West, however, women are channelled into the 'pink sector' of clerical and administrative work. Even graduate women must often start work as secretaries in certain professions (media, publishing), while men gain direct employment to professional posts.

Tragically, it is during wartime periods that women can get the chance to prove themselves. In Britain, for example, they were called up to work in the fields or heavy industry. A third of the

Tigrayan People's Liberation Front consisted of arms-bearing women, and their presence as fighters, not cooks, has had a profound effect on women's status in the region ever since.

> 'Forget positive discrimination; women should get by on merit.'

Women don't want their skills belittled, yet for centuries men have benefited from their own positive discrimination, and kept women in positions below their level of ability. Today, male economic and workplace structures continue to encourage the careers of men to the detriment of equally qualified women. For many women, the only way to reach their full employment potential is to branch out on their own.

> 'Jesus and his disciples were all men.'

In the male-dominated Jewish society of first-century Jerusalem, Jesus would have made little impact had he been born female. Women, though, feature strongly in the Gospels in the accounts of individual lives that God touched. At a time when women were regarded as subordinate to the male of the species (a tradition that both Church and society held strongly well into this century), Jesus treated women with true respect.

ACTION COUNTDOWN

'Securing the equality of women and men, in law and in fact, is the great political project of the 20th century.'

Dr Boutros Boutros-Ghali, 1992–6 Secretary
General of the United Nations.

- **Look at how women are portrayed in magazines, papers, on television, in advertisements, films . . .**
  Think about the messages being given out to women – and men – by these images.
- **Read about women's issues across the world.**
  Resource and information packs on women are available from most Third World charities.

- **Watch** *Rosie the Riveter* – **on women's war work** – **on video.**
  Show it to friends and discuss the issues it raises about women's work.
- **Compare all work done by the different sexes within your household.**
  Work to address any imbalances between the sexes.
- **Compare jobs, qualifications, experience and pay of both sexes at work.**
  Raise any unjust practices with your personnel officer, staff forum, or trade union representative.
- **Compare men's and women's contributions to your church life.**
  Consider the message that this communicates to the local community.
- **Consider how your church celebrates Mothering Sunday.**
  Does it emphasize the Church as Mother? Or simply serve to alienate childless women?
- **Start a Women's Group in your church to talk and pray about women's issues.**
  Consider women in the Church, local community, the nation, and world-wide.
- **Celebrate Women's International Day of Prayer.**
  Contact women in other local churches to pray together on the first Friday of March.
- **Work to change structures that keep women in subordinate roles.**
  Campaign for childcare facilities, nursery places, flexitime at work, above-benefit rates of pay for part-time work (the only people who can presently afford to do most jobshares are those with a working partner), equal pay and value of skills and qualifications.

MAKING CONTACT

Catholic Women's League, 164 Stockwell Road, LONDON SW9.
  Tel: 0171 738 4894.
Mothers' Union, Mary Sumner House, 24 Tufton Street, LONDON
  SW1P 3RB. Tel: 0171 222 5533.
National Federation of Women's Institutes,
  104 New Kings Road, LONDON SW6. Tel: 0171 371 9300.

UN Division for the Advancement of Women, Room DC2 1220, United Nations, New York, NY 10017, USA.

Women's Aid Federation, PO Box 391, BRISTOL BS99 7WS. Tel: 0117 944 4411. (*National Helpline*: 0345 023468.)

Women's Environmental Network (WEN): *see* **E–ENVIRONMENT**.

Women's World Day of Prayer, Commercial Road, TONBRIDGE, Kent. Tel: 01892 541411.

GAMBLING

'Just as a Christian offers himself, his soul and body to be a living sacrifice, so he also places the resources entrusted to him, not least his income, at God's disposal.'

Simon Webley, from his book *Money Matters* (IVP, 1978)

Facts of the matter

- The odds on winning the UK National Lottery jackpot are 14 million to 1.
- In the first year of the National Lottery, there were 127 lottery millionaires. Nationally, £4.4 billion was spent on lottery tickets.
- Only 5.6p of every £1 spent on a National Lottery ticket goes to charity; 22.4p in every £1 is spent on arts, sports and heritage projects, as well as the Millennium Fund.
- Of the £125 million in Arts Council awards to London venues, 95 per cent of those that benefited were national – such as the Tate Gallery or the Royal Opera House.
- Of the first £40 million distributed by the National Lottery Charities Board, London's 30,000 charities received only 3.9 per cent.[1]

Introduction

Gambling has had a constant place in human history. People have always sought out the opportunity to gain a quick profit from investment in a 'surefire bet', whether that be in the world's financial markets, or by putting money on a horse in the hope that it will cross the finishing line first. Even tossing the coin at the start of a sports match is a gamble.

Risk and taking a gamble reflect the very nature of life. Without some risk, human beings cannot grow, as any child learning to walk soon realizes. Many engineering feats and heroic achievements only occurred because people were prepared to risk much, sometimes even their lives. It is healthy to stretch ourselves, to challenge our fears, to grow, but it must go hand in hand with commonsense. The odds of danger to ourselves and others must be taken into account – and minimized.

Gambling *money* is another matter, though. The odds are heavily stacked against the punter; they must put their trust in chance. That is not to say nobody can win – John Aspinall funded his wildlife parks via gambling, and there are poker players whose winning streaks are down to good memory and skill at the game. However, those Lloyd's names who thought they had placed a safe bet got their fingers severely burnt when the insurance boat came in. Not only is gambling a fairly certain way of wasting the financial resources God has put at our disposal – and therefore irresponsible – but the emphasis on *chance* negates putting our faith in a Lord who ordains our life path.

Also, gambling offers people a false hope. It is a commercial venture heavily stacked in favour of those who organize it; it is not in their interests for winning to be easy. For example, the National Lottery's 'roll over' weeks, which draw out further millions of gamblers to buy tickets, show just how difficult the National Lottery jackpot is to win! And while many an individual's antipathy towards it is contradicted by their own gambling on financial markets, or gaming with a veneer of skill attached (such as horse-racing or the football pools), the National Lottery has its own place in history. Overnight, the British government signalled to its people that their hope for a better life was a matter of pure chance. It *could* be you.

> 'If I win anything, I'll donate something to charity.'

Promises made *before* betting and winning can change once the money is handed over to you. Already there are reports of syndicates breaking down (though provision can be made to prevent this) and of long-term relationships of family, friends and workmates being devastated when an individual decides not to be as generous as they once boasted they would be prior to winning.

Charities have seen a downfall in donations since the introduction of the National Lottery, for those with loose change in their pockets are choosing to spend it on a ticket rather than put it in a collecting tin as they once did. People are also telling themselves that having a flutter on the National Lottery is an alternative way of giving to charity, though in reality only 5.6p of every £1 goes to charities – and many charities get no cut at all.

> 'Winning so much money would ruin anybody.'

While winning the 'big one' would be a shock to anyone's system, this argument is surely as much related to jealousy, class and the Protestant work ethic. We can all cite cases where money clearly didn't buy happiness – perhaps the Getty family, James Blandford, Howard Hughes, Michael Jackson – but nobody turns to nice Paul and Linda McCartney, Richard Branson, Cliff Richard or Sting and says, 'It must be tough being a millionaire'!

Having much money tends to reveal the person we truly are, rather than change us. With no need to worry about financial security, those with money are able to buy any lifestyle they choose – and that will ultimately say more about them than cash ever can.

> 'It's only a bit of harmless fun.'

For people with money to throw away, gambling can seem like a bit of a lark, but for families financially dependent on an individual who is *addicted* to betting, or people living in poverty who place their life's hope on winning, the truth is very different. The reality about gambling is that for the most part few people, even so-called expert tabloid pundits, ever win more money than they pay out. The National Lottery is in effect a tax on those who indulge, privatizing many people's sense of hopelessness, and using their money for causes that *everybody* could contribute to via National Insurance.

> 'Gambling isn't Christian.'

Gambling is a waste of the financial resources given to us by God. It is a pursuit that relies more on chance than his graciousness; in the same way that we cannot pray to him to change our exam results, God will not alter the numbers on our tickets or the colour of the cards in our hand. God has better things to do with our money.

Yet many Christians do have an occasional flutter. The Catholic weekly *The Universe* has racing tips on its back page, and many Anglican churches have prize draws and raffles to raise funds. It is ultimately something we have to weigh up for ourselves, to consider the greater good. Christians should be able to give without expecting anything in return, but there are occasions – at the office or pub, for example – where money is being raised for a good cause via the selling of raffle tickets. To refuse to buy a ticket on the basis of principle can send out a killjoy message about the Christian faith, though in such cases simply making a donation, or giving away any prize you do win, are possible options.

ACTION COUNTDOWN

> *'No servant can serve two masters: for either he will hate the one, and love the other; or else he will hold to the one, and despise the other. Ye cannot serve God and mammon.'*
>
> Jesus Christ

- **Treat money with care.**
  Thank God for the money entrusted to you – and use it for his glory.
- **Just say 'no'.**
  If you find gambling becoming a habit, turn and walk away. Or seek help.
- **Save the money you would spend on the National Lottery.**
  Put aside at least £1 a week for a good cause of your choosing.
- **Spend thoughtfully any money you do win.**
  If you do win on the Grand National or whatever, spread some happiness by buying presents.
- **Identify those without financial hope in your area.**
  Look out for young single mothers and hard-up pensioners, and help them out.
- **Collect for charity outside your local bookmakers.**
  Rattle a tin – or carol sing – and make good use of people's loose change.

- **Have a prize draw that people have a chance of winning.**
  Pool local finances via a raffle, and put the money back into the community.
- **Identify a local community need and start a collection.**
  Encourage church members to give, expecting nothing in return.
- **Campaign for better social services.**
  For many of the nation's poor, the National Lottery seems their only real hope for a change in lifestyle. Act politically to make a difference to their lack of choice.
- **Spread the Good News.**
  Life is more than chance, and God is more than a faceless 'Big Finger'. Tell people of Jesus' love for them – and how he gives purpose to life. Show people you care through Christian actions.

MAKING CONTACT

Credit Action, 6 Regent Terrace, CAMBRIDGE CB2 1AA.
   Tel: 01223 324034. (*Helpline available.*)
Gamblers Anonymous: Tel: 0171 384 3040.
Gamcare (National Association for Gambling Care, Educational
   Resources and Training), Suite 1, Catherine House, 25–27
   Catherine Place, LONDON SW1E 6DU. Tel: 0171 233 8988.
National Lottery Line: Tel: 0645 100 000.
Overcomers: Tel: 01344 50736.

Risk is Freedom

To laugh is to risk appearing the fool

To weep is to risk appearing sentimental

To reach out for another is to risk involvement

To express feeling is to risk exposing your true self

To place your ideas, your dreams, before a crowd is to
risk their loss

To love is to risk not being loved in return

To live is to risk dying

To hope is to risk despair

To try is to risk failure

But risks must be taken because the greatest hazard in
life is to risk nothing

The person who risks nothing does nothing, has nothing,
is nothing

He may avoid suffering and sorrow but he cannot learn,
change, feel, grow, love, live

Chained by the certitude he has forfeited his freedom

Only a person who risks is free.

Anonymous

HOMELESSNESS

'Christians cannot accept the present high levels of home-lessness. Every person has the right to a home where they can live securely and develop their God-given abilities.'

Statement by UNLEASH (Church Action on
Homelessness in London)

Facts of the matter

- UK households declared as homeless rose from 249,100 in 1986 to 339,400 in 1993.
- About 300,000 homes were repossessed in the 5 years to the end of 1994.[1]
- In the year to the end of March 1996, 46,290 homeowners suffered repossessions.[2]
- Tonight, 8,000 people will sleep rough in city centres, towns, villages, seaside resorts and rural areas throughout the UK. Another 60,000 will find a bed in a temporary hostel or nightshelter. Thousands more will sleep on a friend's floor or in a squat.[3]
- Housing benefit for single people under 60 is set at the level of the cost of a room in a shared house.
- Approximately 50 per cent of 150 daily calls received by London group Women's Aid are from victims of domestic violence waiting to be rehoused. The 1985 Housing Act entitles them to immediate housing, but many local authorities demand proof of assault.[4]
- Some 10,000 Ministry of Defence properties stand empty, but 25 per cent of homeless people are ex-armed forces.
- According to coroners' records, the average age of death of a homeless person is 47 years.
- According to the homelessness body Crisis, about 600 people die every year while living on UK streets.
- Around 30 per cent of the total number of homeless people in London are aged over 50.[5]

- About 80 per cent of street people in London aged over 60 had been sleeping rough for 5 years or more.[6]

Introduction

Homelessness has always been present in British society, but in recent years the problem has grown dramatically. Changes of attitudes in society, government policy, and the present economic situation have made having a home less of a certainty for us all.

Public expenditure on housing has fallen in recent decades and the problem exacerbated by the Conservative government's 'right to buy' policy for council house tenants. The stock of houses sold off has yet to be replaced to help those desperately in need of accommodation. People are forced to rent poorly kept accommodation – living in 'bed and breakfasts', and having to walk the streets during the day. People from ethnic minorities represent many of the 'hidden homeless' – those who live in vastly over-crowded conditions where illness can spread rapidly, or sleep on people's floors rather than in shop doorways.

Recession and job losses forced millions of people to suffer repossessions after falling behind on mortgage repayments, many of whom had stretched their credit to the limit during the 1980s consumer boom. Elsewhere, properties that could be converted into low-cost homes – like empty office blocks or so-called redundant hospital buildings – were left empty or were demolished, often to make way for expensive new private housing estates.

> 'Aren't those people who beg all con artists?'

Probably to the extent that people who work in the City of London are all fraudsters! Within any chosen group of people, there will always be a percentage who are dishonest. However, sitting outside in the cold and damp all day with a piece of battered card that reads 'Homeless and Hungry' seems a pretty half-hearted and inefficient attempt to defraud the public.

> 'Surely home life isn't that bad?'

Passers-by often wonder whether the teenagers they see begging would not be better off back at the family home. However, most children seen begging will have grown up in local authority care. Once they get to 18, they no longer have to be housed and automatically become homeless. For the victims of child abuse, leaving home may be the only escape from a nightmare world. Even some universities have had to set up soup kitchens during vacations for students with no home to go to: their middle-class parents delayed splitting up until 'the children left home', term-time addresses have closed, and students cannot claim housing benefit to tide them over.

'Can't they get themselves a proper job?'

Finding work at school-leaving age is hard, and the government will only provide support if young people enrol on Youth Training and Employment programmes administered by local businesses. Yet in areas of high unemployment there may be no training places available. With no access to benefit, teenagers in depressed areas are particularly vulnerable since they bring in no income to their already hard-pressed families. They may be pressurized to leave home in search of work, without any financial support.

The 'Catch 22' of getting a job is that you have to have a proper address. To be able to afford the money for the deposit on rented accommodation, you need a job. Homeless people of any age cannot obtain bank or building society accounts, so saving a deposit is almost impossible.

A quarter of homeless people are ex-armed forces. Historically, during post-war periods, soldiers have not necessarily had homes to which they could return. Recent redundancies among a workforce for whom a home goes with the job, combined with personalities used to living under a strict regime, makes it hard to adjust to the relatively relaxed nature of civilian life where accommodation is not a right.

'Shouldn't these people be receiving some
sort of treatment?'

The Conservative government's Care in the Community programme aimed to release mentally disabled people from large, isolated and outdated Victorian institutions, but little was done to ensure adequate provision of suitable housing and qualified people to support them. Many ended up on the streets, unable to look after themselves. For those dependent on prescribed medication to remain mentally stable, it can be difficult to stick to the correct dosage without supervision, and their condition quickly deteriorates.

> 'Why do we have to put up with these people
> on the streets anyway?'

Some people would rather the pavements were lifted up and the beggars and the homeless swept under them. In London's Strand, hoteliers chose to wash down the street to prevent people sleeping out. Later, then Shadow Home Secretary Jack Straw angered housing charities *and* human rights groups when he effectively declared war on 'winos, addicts and squeegee merchants', whose begging bothered 'decent, law-abiding citizens'.

In other countries, unwanted groups of people – such as street children – are simply annihilated. In some British cities, beggars are banned. People in this country working on behalf of the mentally ill have pointed out that government policy in real terms means that people have simply been let out into the streets to die. Unless there is a determined national social programme to care for vulnerable people, there will be plenty more casualties – many of them members of the soaring elderly population – unable to fend for themselves physically or financially. If we begin to wonder at the increase in the number of homeless people, our questioning must lead to active compassion for this community.

ACTION COUNTDOWN

'I tell you the truth, whatever you did not do for one of the least of these, you did not do for me.'
Jesus Christ

- **Buy a copy of** *The Big Issue*, **the magazine sold by homeless people.**
  The trained vendor keeps part of the cover price of each copy sold.

47

- **Buy a cup of coffee or some food for the next person you see begging in the street.**
  Break down barriers by giving someone food or a hot drink, or treat them to a meal.
- **Take food with you to distribute whenever you go out.**
  Carry chocolate, a packed lunch, fruit or spare change to give away.
- **Donate an hour's pay to the next homeless person you meet.**
  Or do something to raise money quickly (busk, hold a sale, or baby-sit) and give with love.
- **Befriend a homeless person.**
  If you see individuals regularly, exchange greetings and, if they allow, get to know them.
- **Visit a 'homeless' person in their 'home'.**
  Help make it a liveable space; seek to change bad housing practice too.
- **Find out where the local hostels, shelters and day centres are.**
  When you come across someone obviously in need of help, it is vital to know where such hostels are.
- **Encourage your church to become involved in helping homeless people.**
  Collect food from members of the congregation, local shops, restaurants for local hostels and centres, provide meals on a regular basis and a place to shelter, or even establish a hostel.
- **Volunteer for a Salvation Army or Crisis soup or clothing run.**
  The need is constant. The work is tough and cold, but *very* rewarding.
- **Invite a homeless person home to stay or share a pot of tea.**
  With regard to your own safety, follow your instincts about helping a particular person, and trust in God. People will see the difference that your faith makes.

MAKING CONTACT

Centrepoint, Bewlay House, 2 Swallow Place, LONDON W1R 7AA. Tel: 0171 629 2229.

CHAR, 5–15 Cromer Street, LONDON WC1H 8LS. Tel: 0171 833 2071.

CHAS (Catholic Housing Aid Society), 209 Old Marylebone Road, LONDON NW1 5QT. Tel: 0171 723 7273.

Church Housing Trust, Sutherland House, 70–78 West Hendon Broadway, LONDON NW9 7BT. Tel: 0181 203 9233.

Churches National Housing Coalition (CNHC), Central Buildings, Oldham Street, MANCHESTER M1 1JY. Tel: 0161 236 9321.

Crisis, 1st floor, Challenger House, 42 Adler Street, LONDON E1 1EE. Tel: 0171 377 0489.

Shelter, 88 Old Street, LONDON EC1V 9HU. Tel: 0171 253 0202.

UNLEASH (Church Action on Homelessness in London), Trinity House, 4 Chapel Court, Borough High Street, LONDON SE1 1HW.

INVESTMENT

'Ethical investment seeks to invest in companies which make a positive contribution to society, and avoid those which harm the world or its people.'

Friends Provident Stewardship, the UK's first ethical investment fund, launched June 1984

Facts of the matter

- Only 21 per cent of the British population have heard of the term 'ethical investment'.
- Upon receiving a clear definition of ethical investment, 94 per cent of a sample of 1,000 adults agreed: 'I want my investment to benefit companies which are helping rather than harming the world', and 92 per cent said that they would like to profit without hurting anyone.[1]
- A third of world trade consists of internal transactions within individual multinational companies.[2]
- According to the Ethical Investment Research and Information Service (EIRIS), funds invested in ethical and Green unit trusts increased by more than 17 per cent between June 1991 and June 1992 compared with an increase of only 3 per cent in the total amount invested in unit trusts generally during the same period.
- Some $9 billion of US stock exchange investments consist of ethically screened stocks.[3]
- As well as hundreds of companies in Europe and North America, around 40 per cent of companies on the FT-SE All Share Index have been approved by Friends Provident.

Introduction

During the past decade, British culture has been dominated by market values, with even such areas as medicine or education developing strategies of profit-making, and charging for all but the most basic of services. Interestingly, at the same time, the rise of ethical investment – putting your money where your cares are – has also been sharp. Investors can follow their consciences, rather than allowing decisions to be dominated by nothing more than the possibility of making more money.

For Christians with the privilege of having spare money to invest, there is good opportunity via the financial world to make a positive contribution to the local and global community. There is now a wealth of companies that promote investment in community, environmental or developmental business concerns. This is caring capitalism; the investor receives a return on his or her money, while knowing that it has been put to good use.

It was in the 1920s that the Methodist Church in America overturned its attitude towards the stock market as a form of gambling, and chose to invest in companies that had nothing to do with alcohol or gambling. A half-century later, in 1971, the Pax World Fund was set up to promote investment outside the weapons industry as a financial protest against the Vietnam War. On this side of the Atlantic, it was not until 1984 that the Quaker-originated Friends Provident launched its Stewardship Unit Trust.

Today, the concept of 'ethical investment' is sturdy enough for the high street Co-operative Bank to promote itself purely on that basis. Recognizing that money makes the world go round, it uses its power as a bank to choose to whom it lends. By holding money back from companies that do business with oppressive regimes, for example, it exerts pressure for change. Other financial institutions invest only in what are termed 'social economy' businesses: co-operatives, development trusts, and voluntary, community, social or Green businesses that are purely environmentally or socially beneficial. Particularly in run-down communities, such companies offer real hope. They address local needs and make use of local skills and resources in areas where industry has pulled out, resulting in large-scale redundancies, or where full-time employment has always been scarce.

Ethical investment is no passing fad, but provides a real chance for Christians to use their money wisely and make a financial stand for God's value system.

| 'Isn't this "opting out" all a bit negative?' |

Negative business practices (weapons manufacture, animal testing, the production of unsafe products or services, pornography) are set against positives (equal opportunities, good customer and supplier relations, pollution control, the production of quality products of long-term benefit to the community). However, constant review and refinement are vital. New concerns emerge, and world events have consequences – South Africa, once avoided because of its apartheid system, now needs financial help. Investors must take account of latest holdings and dealings; the ethical Friends Provident Stewardship Income Fund invests in RTB mining, the company that bought most of British Coal's English pits.

| 'Is this really responsible use of my money?' |

Investors are often concerned that their money might earn less than if invested in conventional funds – in other words, that a cleaner conscience pays less dividend. However, within a year of its launch in 1984, the Friends Provident Stewardship Income Fund outperformed most of its purely money-oriented rivals, a trend still apparent among the thirty or so funds now available.

Investing ethically makes sound business sense both for individual savers, and for treasurers with the responsibility for managing other people's money. Also, an economic world that squanders the planet's limited resources will eventually be *forced* to be more responsible. Therefore those who invest in companies that take stock of their practices *now* will have chosen good long-term investments, not only for themselves, but for the environment and society as a whole.

| 'Shouldn't there be limits to even ethical growth?' |

Most people invest in order to receive some financial reward for business *growth*; so, at one level, ethical investment offers little real challenge to an economic system that keeps two-thirds of the world trapped in poverty and threatens the future survival of the planet.

In the neglected poorer regions, though, *regenerative* small-scale investment provides the best hope for the future. Where the high street banks have pulled out, it is imperative that support is provided for communities to re-establish themselves via self-sustaining projects.

> 'Whether ethical or not, aren't investors basically out for themselves?'

Up to a third of people would invest ethically at the risk of a lower return on their money, yet its relative success also encourages greed. Some funds – for example, the Ethical Investors Group – give some profit away, yet others promote their portfolio's money-making potential.

There have always been investors who have put their money behind projects they believed to be worthwhile. Ethical enterprises, such as ones promoting ecological development or socially responsible housing schemes, deserve backing. And while the investor's interest might not be totally altruistic, the money they generate might be put to good use.

> 'Isn't this just another form of gambling?'

Some Christians avoid financial investment, since not only is any money earned because they have *bet* on a chosen company's progress, but also because companies end up serving their shareholders and top executives rather than the people who use their products, or their employees. Christians need to consider such practices before they invest their money.

Yet while some Christians will join a trade union in solidarity with their fellow employees in the fight for decent working practices, others will become shareholders to support a vital project. Some Christians, especially in the USA, invest in multinationals that have few ethical concerns, and use their shareholding power to try and steer companies towards more God-honouring endeavours. In the UK, it is harder for shareholders to be so effective, but ethical investment directly encourages those companies that are already working a better way.

ACTION COUNTDOWN

'The ultimate purpose of industry is, I believe, to serve our fellow human beings by creating goods and services to meet their needs. It is not to make money for its own sake.'

George Carey, Archbishop of Canterbury

- **Start saving for a rainy day.**
  Put your spare change to one side, and time aside to decide what to do with your finances.
- **Watch** *It's a Wonderful Life, The Man in the White Suit,* **or** *Wall Street.*
  Alone or with friends, consider the industrial/investment ethics portrayed in these films.
- **Make a list of the ethical issues that you value.**
  Contact EIRIS, the Ethical Investment Research and Information Service.
- **Open an account with the Co-operative Bank.**
  The Co-operative Bank is the first high street bank to promote itself as an ethical investor.
- **Transfer current investments into ethical funds.**
  Make the switch so that your money does less damage.
- **Give without taking anything financial in return.**
  Let your reward be the help you give to communities and small worthwhile businesses.
- **Invite a speaker on ethical investment to your church or workplace.**
  Help to spread the word to those who may find they are interested in the concept.
- **Consider the ethical choices you make in your own everyday dealings.**
  Aim to tread more lightly on the Earth – and its people via the products you buy and use.
- **Work to see that your church and workplace become ethical investors.**
  Raise the issue at relevant meetings so that change can be made for the better.
- **Set up a community 'bank' at your church.**
  Plough the money back into the community and use it to help those struggling financially.

MAKING CONTACT

Christian Ethical Investment Group, 90 Booker Avenue, Bradwell Common, MILTON KEYNES, Buckinghamshire MK13 8EF.

Barchester Green Investment, Barchester House, 45/49 Catherine Street, SALISBURY WHS SP1 2DH. Tel: 01722 331241.

Co-operative Bank, Head of Public Affairs, 1 Balloon Street, MANCHESTER M60 4EP. Tel: 0800 90 50 90.

Ethical Investment Research Service (EIRIS), 504 Bondway Business Centre, 71 Bondway, LONDON SW8 1SQ. Tel: 0171 735 1351.

Ethical Investors Group, Milestone, Greet Road, Greet, CHELTENHAM GL54 5BG. Tel: 01242 522872.

Friends Provident, Pixham End, DORKING, Surrey RH4 1QA. Tel: 01306 740123.

Holden Meehan, 11th floor, Clifton Heights, Triangle West, Clifton, BRISTOL BS8 1EJ. Tel: 0117 9252874.

ICOF Community Capital Limited, 12–14 Gold Street, NORTHAMPTON NN1 1RS. Tel: 01604 37563.

Jupiter Environmental Research Unit, Knightsbridge House, 197 Knightsbridge, LONDON SW7 1RB. Tel: 0171 412 0703.

New Economics Foundation, 1st floor, Vine Court, 112–116 Whitechapel Road, LONDON E1 1JE. Tel: 0171 377 5696.

JUSTICE

'It is not possible to meet with the God of justice and care nothing about injustice. It is not possible to be open to the love of God, and remain indifferent to other people.'

The Reverend Philip Crowe, author of
A Whisper Will Be Heard (Fount, 1994)

Introduction

From an early age, human beings seem to have an innate sense of justice. 'That's not fair' is a cry to be heard in most primary school playgrounds. Many adults remember the dark childhood moment when they first realized a parent had lied to them – an infant coming-of-age when the world was no longer quite what it had seemed. The first recognition of injustice makes a similarly disturbing impact. Who knows whether a childhood slight might not be the impetus for many who choose to fight injustices when they reach adulthood?

The world is an unjust place, where working to right wrongs can be an exhausting and potentially soul-destroying task. In the fight against structural injustices we face the danger of becoming worn down by bitterness and an overwhelming feeling of impotence. Yet, as Christians, it is surely our duty to take our stand alongside those who have been wronged, both in our locality and across the world. By looking towards God for inspiration, individuals learn to realize that an act done in Jesus' name, however small, can have a knock-on effect of great magnitude. It is an act of will and defiance against the evil ties that bind this world. Fighting for justice is not an easy option, but it is one that God will enlighten, and for which he will give each one of us strength. And through it, ultimately, comes true joy.

> 'I can't change the world.'

The late George Hoffman, founder and director of Christian

development agency Tear Fund, had a saying: 'You can't change the world, but you can change the world for one person.' It provides a truly Christian perspective on each individual's ability to make a difference. It is easy to become overwhelmed by the world's needs, but, rather than an excuse for apathy, our knowledge of wrongs should provide motivation to work for at least some small change.

'Isn't charity enough?'

Throughout this book are suggestions for putting love into action, for reaching out to the hungry and the homeless, the lonely and the oppressed. Yet it is not enough simply to give our time, our money, our friendship – though that is certainly of value in itself. True love means encountering people where they are and, in so doing, having our eyes opened to political and social injustices that keep individuals in their impoverished place.

'People who complain about this country are a bunch of "moaning minnies". We're better off than most.'

UK citizens don't live under a dictatorship, the weather is fairly predictable, and there is education for all, a National Health Service, and social security for the unemployed.

Yet despite this, plenty of people are effectively disenfranchised by a parliamentary system that is shifting inexorably to the Right. An 'X' on a piece of paper every four years (that is, if the political party for whom you want to vote is represented in your constituency) allows a government unelected by the majority to change their ways once they are in power. Individual MPs can also switch party mid-term, and not stand down to allow a by-election.

The Welfare State has been deliberately weakened and many people are suffering the consequences of this. Every winter, elderly people die of hypothermia because they cannot afford high fuel bills. In bad weather, people on low incomes and without insurance may be left homeless when freak floods occur. The Criminal Justice Bill turned travelling families into criminals overnight, and illegalized spontaneous celebrations and demonstrations. There is no right to silence, the police can stop and search whom they choose, and security cameras watch us in our cities. The UK may be better off than most, but it is in no way perfect.

| 'Christianity and politics shouldn't mix.' |

Christians involved in social and/or political action are often accused by both fellow believers and those against whom they take a stand as being more concerned with the earthly here-and-now than the spiritual realms of the hereafter. This division, though, is not reflected in Jesus' teachings.

> *'It is true that the poor in Latin America are materialistic. Without bread, housing and medicine, they die. It is true that Christians in South Africa are concerned with politics, for the oppression of black people is political. It is true that Christians who press for the redistribution of wealth can sometimes sound like Marxists. But such political materialism is an expression of faith, not a denial of it.'*
>
> The Reverend Philip Crowe,
> author of *A Whisper Will Be Heard* (Fount, 1994)

ACTION COUNTDOWN

> *'Solidarity, principles, analysis, action, all are essential in working for justice.'*
> The Reverend Philip Crowe, author of
> *A Whisper Will Be Heard* (Fount, 1994)

- **Keep informed.**
  Read a quality newspaper, and watch television programmes on current affairs and social change.
- **Pray for God to open your eyes.**
  Ask God to show you on which of the world's problems he wants you to concentrate.
- **Become an 'expert'.**
  Build up a contacts list and archive of cuttings and books covering your favourite concern.

- **Remain humble and do not judge.**
  A little learning can be a dangerous thing; it's easy to become superior about what you now know and what others may not yet have grasped. Hand all you have, and all you are, to God.
- **Write to your MP.**
  Politely express your own views, and ask for the issue to be raised in the House of Commons.
- **Write to the newspapers.**
  Free local papers are an especially good forum. Respond to relevant news stories presenting a just and Christian perspective on the matter. Write to the national newspapers too.
- **Join a pressure group.**
  Network with like-minded people at a national and local level.
- **Unite with Christians who feel the same way as you do.**
  Provide prayer and pastoral support to each other in the tough fight against injustice.
- **Take matters into your own hands.**
  Become actively involved in making a difference. Think of what needs to be done, and do it.
- **Stand for office.**
  Follow Jesus' servant style of leadership, and humbly put yourself forward for a parish, council or constituency seat.

MAKING CONTACT

Charter 88, Exmouth House, 3–11 Pine Street, LONDON EC1R 0JH. Tel: 0171 833 1988. (*Phoneline*: 0891 34 56 88.)

Christians for Social Justice, 31 Prince of Wales Lane, Yardley Wood, BIRMINGHAM B14 4LB.

National Council for Civil Liberties, 21 Tabard Street, LONDON SE1 4LA. Tel: 0171 403 3888.

First they came for the Jews
and I did not speak out –
because I was not a Jew.

Then they came for the Communists
and I did not speak out –
because I was not a Communist.

Next they came for the Trade Unionists
and I did not speak out –
because I was not a Trade Unionist.

Then they came for me
and there was no one left
to speak out for me.

Pastor Niemoeller, victim of the Holocaust

KINGDOM

'The "kingdom of heaven" is the rule of God and is both a present reality and a future hope.'

New International Version Study Bible

Introduction

God's Kingdom is not purely a New World Order for which we must wait until the end of time. Certainly the Christian hope is in a place where there is no darkness and only Light exists, where suffering, poverty, danger and fear are no more, but in the same way that eternity has already begun, Jesus' promise that he would bring life more abundant begins now.

That is not to say that as Christians our life paths will be smooth, and that we will not suffer hardship, pain, illness or sudden bereavement in the same way as anyone else. But we do so knowing that Jesus is by our side and that we are not alone, and therefore experience something of the heavenly togetherness with God that is to come.

As creator of the universe and 'great king over all the earth' (Psalm 24), God has not left it to its own devices, though he has given us choice to work for or against him. In the person of Jesus came our salvation, and a human being made perfect, whose ways we are to follow. In the Holy Spirit we have an internal spiritual guide who draws us towards God.

Though for the time being we are limited by our earthly humanity, redemption for us as individuals has already begun. Similarly, God's non-human creation experiences the desire for complete fulfilment, groaning for the time when it will be made whole (Romans 8.22).

Our job, then, as earthly ambassadors is to work for the glory of God. In so doing, our achievements and the relationships that develop will hint at the heavenly Kingdom that is promised to all who put their hand in his.

> 'Surely this world will pass away? God's
> Kingdom is a different place.'

Jesus spoke much about the Kingdom of God; the sense of an otherworldly style of rule lies at the centre of his teaching. At Jesus' trial, the confused Pontius Pilate asked whether indeed the accused was the 'King of the Jews', and Jesus hinted that his Kingdom was outside human comprehension. The Kingdom of God is where God is ruler, and therefore for Christians it began at the moment when they committed their lives to him. Yet it is also a true and beautiful future hope.

> 'Why bother trying to change things?
> All will be redeemed in heaven.'

The Christian's hope of eternal glory to be encountered in heaven can inspire believers to do great things for God or, conversely, do nothing. If this world is to pass away, then any moves to make a difference can ultimately seem pointless. Taken to its logical conclusion, we could perversely argue that it is futile being treated for a life-threatening illness, or providing facilities for disabled people, since everything will eventually be made whole.

Jesus' ministry was a true expression of the Kingdom of God in the here-and-now. Similarly, our actions done to glorify God become sanctified and have eternal resonance. Jesus advised us to store up our treasures in heaven instead of spending time on accumulating earthly possessions. Therefore any positive action done in his name is pure gold.

> 'If God is King, doesn't that make us
> princes and princesses?'

There is good reason to wonder why so many Christians are shy and retiring, submissive and low in self-esteem, when they happen to be paid-up members at the court of God's holy realm.

Christians should be strong of heart and fearless, ready for battle in God's name. In the same way that we know that we are loved and beautiful in God's sight, we can also rightly tell ourselves that royal blood courses through our veins. We have reason to hold our heads up high.

> ## 'Isn't our job here to follow earthly rulers and authority?'

Christians are called to be good citizens, to be a strong presence within society, but while many churches across the world pray for those in power, ultimately our allegiance must be with God. It can often be more Christian to disobey the earthly powers.

To lead lives of integrity we must be true to what we believe is God's call for our lives. It is not enough simply to serve our earthly rulers; we must keep watch at all times, and with wisdom discern the way of the world. Through God's guidance, and our intelligence about historical patterns and human nature, we should be able to tell in advance which way the wind will blow. For Christians to follow the world's paths to positive change or to folly is to be too late. Our role should be to lead along a path of justice and righteousness.

ACTION COUNTDOWN

'Thy Kingdom come, thy will be done, on earth as it is in Heaven.'

Matthew 6:10

- **For a month, collect magazine and newspaper articles about the world's royal families.**
  Consider the positive and negative traits revealed. What is godly about their behaviour?
- **Read Matthew 13 on the parable of the sower and the seed.**
  Recall how an act of love you once did had positive knock-on effects.
- **Look up the word 'Kingdom' in a Bible concordance.**
  Read the references listed.
- **Meditate on the image you now have of God's Kingdom.**
  Consider what you can do in your everyday life to reveal something of what you have learnt.
- **Begin with yourself.**
  Make ethical choices about the clothes you wear, and the cosmetics and toiletries you use.

- **Make honesty your watchword.**
  Develop integrity in all that you say and do.
- **Open your home to others.**
  Make your living space a place where people will feel comfortable, respected and loved.
- **Bring the love of God into your workplace.**
  Make your workspace a place where people will feel comfortable, respected and loved.
- **Find a rundown building or piece of land and work to improve it.**
  Begin to help rebuild God's shattered world in practical ways.
- **Support projects such as home-help services, bereavement counselling, or citizens' advice groups that help rebuild shattered lives.**
  In our local communities and throughout the world, an awful lot of people are living lives of silent despair under brutal conditions. Be at their side.

MAKING CONTACT

British Trust for Conservation Volunteers:
See **E – ENVIRONMENT.**
CARE: *See* **B – BODY POLITICS.**
Charity People Employment Agency, Station House,
150 Waterloo Road, LONDON SE1 8SB. Tel: 0171 636 3900.
Christian Impact, St Peter's Church, Vere Street, LONDON
W1M 9HP. Tel: 0171 629 3615.
Christian Vocations, Holloway Street West, Lower Gornal,
DUDLEY, West Midlands DY3 2DZ. Tel: 01902 882836.
Community Service Volunteers, 237 Pentonville Road, LONDON
N1 9NJ. Tel: 0171 278 6601.
Evangelical Alliance, Whitefield House, 186 Kennington Park
Road, LONDON SE11 4BT. Tel: 0171 207 2100.
  - 3 Fitzwilliam Street, BELFAST BT9 6AW. Tel: 01232 247920.
  - 20 High Street, CARDIFF CF1 2BZ. Tel: 01222 229822.
  - Challenge House, 29 Canal Street, GLASGOW G4 0AD.
    Tel: 0141 332 8700.

National Association of Volunteer Bureaux, New Oxford House, Waterloo Street, BIRMINGHAM B2 5UG. Tel: 0121 633 4555.

Samaritans. 0345 90 90 90.

Scripture Union: *See* **C – CHILDREN**.

Skillshare Africa, Ceresole House, 53 Regent Road, LEICESTER LE1 6YL. Tel: 01162 541 862.

Sojourners, 12 Roundhay Grove, LEEDS LS8 4DS.

United Nations Association (UN Association), 3 Whitehall Court, LONDON SW1. Tel: 0171 930 2932.

Volunteer Centre UK, Carriage Row, 183 Eversholt Street, LONDON NW1 1BU. Tel: 0171 388 9888.

LETTERS

'In the darkest hours of my imprisonment, your words and cards came as the most welcome drops of rain in an endless desert, your letters and reports as the voice of wisdom and the conscience of the world.'

Mohammed El Boukili, a former prisoner of conscience

Introduction

The power of a well-timed letter through the post cannot be underestimated, and pressure groups such as Amnesty International and the Jubilee Campaign know this. Encouraging supporters to write to their MP, or a foreign embassy, or a prisoner of conscience, is a valuable part of these pressure groups' work. Probably more effective than a petition of signatures, the fact that individuals took the time, trouble and thought to compose a letter to express their concern is a far more strident form of action. A thousand names on a few sheets of paper can be almost dismissed, but a thousand separate letters – whether by post or e-mail – makes a solid impact. And, by definition, a letter also demands some sort of response. Similarly, alone in his Beirut cell, Terry Waite was glad of the postcard of John Bunyan that had been sent by a wellwisher all the way from England. The knowledge that people on the outside *care* about you, and are praying for you, is a great source of comfort and strength.

The ability to write a good letter is something that should not be devalued in our increasingly electronic age. (Indeed, a recent British Telecom advertisement showed a woman phoning her children to remind them to send *cards* to their grandmother for her birthday. Yes, the subtext went, it's good to pick up the phone and *talk*, but it's still appreciated when people *mail* their regards too.) On paper or via the Internet, letter-writing is a cheap and highly effective form of personal communication. It is also something that can be undertaken by virtually anyone, regardless of age, social position, handicap or academic level – though obviously some people will need assistance. By such a simple means, the individual voice may be heard.

> 'Putting pen to paper isn't true action.'

Many social activists regard the quiet, solo pursuit of writing letters as limited, and often ineffective. In contrast, demonstrating, debate and making major changes to one's lifestyle seem like *proper* campaigning work – upfront, and far more likely to bring about positive change.

Admittedly, for those disillusioned with the nation's parliamentary system, it's easy to become sceptical about the point of writing to one's MP. However, an intellligent, well-argued, polite letter, putting a considered point of view, should earn a reply. It may also draw the attention of your MP to an issue to which they'd previously given little if any thought, and which ultimately might be raised in the House of Commons.

> 'My one letter won't make a difference.'

Letter-writing often makes a difference by sheer force of numbers. When the perpetrators of barbarism are aware that people across the world *know* the evil of their ways and reflect it back at them via pertinent letters, pressure to change becomes heavy and real. A letter of complaint to any organization is generally acknowledged as representing a far greater number of people who *didn't* bother to write, but felt the same way. And a letter from one individual to another during a time of trial is a source of love.

> 'You have to be an intellectual to write a letter.'

Certainly if one is campaigning via mail-outs or press releases, then it is vital that you are a good writer. In less formal situations, though, letters are able to reflect the personality and ability of the writer, and as such do not need to be high-brow. A scrawled note from an infant, a few words on the back of a postcard, and an out-of-the blue epistle, all have their place and value in appropriate circumstances. Many disabled people have found themselves liberated via the Internet, by its enabling them to communicate with others without being judged by their handicap.

'Writing letters is old-fashioned.'

There is an unusual war memorial on Platform 1 of London's Paddington Station. Unlike most memorials depicting soldiers, this one is not caught in a moment of armed combat. Rather, he stands at ease, reading a letter from home. Hand-written letters, like books, still have a role to play today. Both are clearly portable, longer-lasting than they first appear and, apart from a source of light, need no artificial power to be accessed. They can be read in some of the world's most out-of-the-way and worst-case scenarios.

For individuals, a personal letter says far more than a much-copied mail-out, though the latter issued from charities and pressure groups has a strong role in calling people to action. And while e-mail sent via the world-wide network is one of the fastest-growing forms of global communication, it requires the use of a telephone – a piece of equipment that half of humanity has never used.

ACTION COUNTDOWN

'In the right hands, a pen is a powerful instrument of change. In your hands it can make things happen. It can get justice.'

Amnesty International

- **Write to friends and relations in faraway places.**
  It's cheap to phone, but a written letter is a joy to discover among the usual junk mail and bills.
- **Write a letter of thanks.**
  The 'thank you' note seems in decline, so one sent with sincerity will be truly appreciated.
- **Write to someone with whom you have lost touch.**
  Break through the time barrier and renew old acquaintances.
- **Write to let people know that their work is appreciated.**
  Write to encourage a writer, actor, speaker or minister, and let them know what you think.
- **Write a letter of complaint.**
  Write to a television company with regard to a programme you

disagree with, an advertisement you find offensive, or perhaps an advertisement promoting an exploitative product.

- **Write to your local newspaper.**
  Use local news stories as a basis for raising wider global issues via the Letters Page.
- **Write press releases for your church or local organizations.**
  If you can write well, use the local press to publicize your group's work.
- **Write to your MP.**
  Voice your concern about local or world issues, and ask to meet him or her for further discussion.
- **Join Amnesty International's letter-writing campaign.**
  Meet with others locally to write to prisoners and their captors across the world.
- **Write to a prisoner on Death Row; contact Lifelines (see the Making Contact section) for details.**
  In the USA, people facing execution in prison often tend to be black, badly educated, mentally disabled or poor; white, middle-class educated criminals can afford good lawyers to argue their case. A letter from outside can be a godsend, but be prepared to correspond for *years* rather than months.

MAKING CONTACT

Advertising Standards Authority, Brook House, 2–16 Torrington Place, LONDON WC1E 7HW. Tel: 0171 580 5555.

Amnesty International, 99–119 Rosebery Avenue, LONDON EC1R 4RE. Tel: 0171 814 6200.

Broadcasting Standards Commission, 7 The Sanctuary, LONDON SW1P 3JS. Tel: 0171 233 0544.

Fraser Steel, Head of the Programmes Complaints Unit BBC, Broadcasting House, LONDON W1A 1AA. Further details: Ceefax p. 678.

House of Commons, Houses of Parliament, Westminster, LONDON SW1A 2PW. Tel: 0171 219 3000.

House of Lords: *see* **House of Commons**.

Independent Television Commission, 33 Foley Street, LONDON W1P 7LB. Tel: 0171 255 3000.

Lifelines, 96 Fallowfield, CAMBRIDGE CB4 1PF. Tel: 0122 3832877.

Press Complaints Commission, 1 Salisbury Square, LONDON EC4Y 8AE. Tel: 0171 353 1248.

Radio Authority, Holbrook House, 14 Great Queen Street, LONDON WC2B 5DG. Tel: 0171 430 2724.

Viewer and Listener Correspondence, BBC, Villiers House, The Broadway, Haven Green, LONDON W5 2PA.
Tel: 0181 743 8000 (television); Tel: 0171 580 4468 (radio).

For further details regarding appropriate television and radio bodies, check the *Write to . . .* column on the Letters Page of the *Radio Times.*

MONEY

'That we should give, and give generously, seems to be required by our Christian faith. That we should give responsibly, only after careful thought and prayer is also required.'

Professor Robin Gill, in the Lent book for 1991,
Gifts of Love (Fount, 1991)

Facts of the matter

- Of the 100 largest economic players in the world today, 51 are multinational companies and 49 are nation states.[1]
- Some 10 million British people are shareholders; this is a drop of 1 million since 1991 when more than 1 in 5 adults held shares in public utilities sold by the Conservative government.
- More than 50 per cent of private investors hold no more than two shares.
- Approximately 65 per cent of all Stock Exchange transactions are carried out by small investors, even though they control just 20 per cent of the entire market.[2]
- About 40 per cent of UK adults own a credit card, and spend an average of £45 each time they use it.
- Approximately 3 million British people get a weekly visit from the debt collector.
- In 1995, £58 billion was spent in the UK using credit cards.
- Excluding mortgages, British people are on average around £1,000 in debt.
- Graduates earn an average £15,000 in their first post-university post, but are on average £8,000 in debt on obtaining their degree.

Introduction

Many people have an ambivalent attitude towards money. While they recognize that it is virtually impossible to function in any society without cash of some sort, it nevertheless remains a subject that they choose not to discuss. It is a subject, though, from which Jesus never shied. He recognized the grip that Mammon can hold on each of our souls. Society would be truly changed for the better if Christians took as much heed of the strong biblical emphasis given to financial responsibilities as they do about sexual ethics, which Jesus mentioned far less often.

While money and the possessions and power it buys can so easily turn us away from God, money also has tremendous potential for good. Additionally, because it is such an intrinsic part of the way the world works, our attitude towards it speaks volumes. To indicate its *lack* of hold over us reveals how we put our trust in God.

> 'The world asks how much we own; Christ asks how we use it. The world thinks more of getting; Christ thinks more of giving. The world asks what we give; Christ asks how we give; the former thinks of the amount, the latter of the motive. To the world, money is a means of gratification; to the Christian, a means of grace: to the one an opportunity of comfort; to the other an opportunity of consecration.'
>
> Simon Webley, in *Money Matters* (IVP, 1978)

Within our vastly materialistic society it is easy to succumb to the 'get rich quick' messages that pressure us daily. A walk along any high street in a town reveals the heart of our society: stores are crammed with goods that nobody really needs. While a certain level of luxury – the giving of nice presents, the thrill of new fashions – is acceptable, the fact that our entire economic system is based on producing more of everything is ultimately foolish. It is neither good for the world nor the human heart. Not only are vital resources squandered in the pursuit of more possessions that add very little to our lives, and nothing to our life's worth, but the very production of such goods, while providing jobs, essentially devalues humanity. Our *raison d'être* is not to acquire more and more material goods; it is to honour and worship God.

> 'Money is morally neutral. It's what you do with it that counts.'

Money is a concept created by humanity and, as such, cannot be neutral. It contains within it the capacity to be used for great good and great evil. By design, it comes between people; economic value is placed on transactions that could be done in the name of love.

Christianity is about giving without expecting anything in return. An economic system is one where everything has a price, and expects something back with interest. It also devalues those things that money cannot buy: good service and manners, or wild open spaces and communal facilities set aside for simple pleasures, lose out to a culture of money-spinning.

> '*I am wealthy because I am richly blessed by God.*'

Most of the world's Christians live in poverty. To equate a Western standard of living with good spiritual health not only implies that Third World believers lack faith, but suggests that our life of over-abundance in a finite world is also of God. Often those who are able to declare that 'I needed a car/highly paid job/home in a nice middle-class suburb/Christian education for my child – and God gave it to me' belong to a class of people who may believe they have a *right* to such things. Others further down the social scale, or with less money, simply go without.

Although God does open doors and leads us to places we would not otherwise have gone, his rich blessings are more often in the spiritual realms than the material world. He opens our eyes to the wonders that he created in our relationships and in the world around us, and his Holy Spirit gently alters our attitudes so that we do not fear material limitations.

> '*Spend, spend, spend. After all, you can't take it with you.*'

The touch of money should not weigh heavy in a Christian's pocket. We should not be foolhardy with it, but it is good to enjoy life, though we must balance our fun-seeking with the needs and happiness of others. Money spent on someone else can bring great pleasure. Jesus' truth that 'it is better to give than receive' conveys the joy to be had in seeing someone's face light up on receiving a gift. Many people are locked into a somewhat justified fear about their future pension needs, health insurance and mortgage payments, which prevents them from being adventurous in life. We need to be responsible, but we can also trust that God will provide.

> 'Jesus didn't mean what he said about the eye
> of the needle.'

'It is harder for a rich man to enter the Kingdom of Heaven, than for a camel to pass through the eye of a needle,' said Jesus, and this statement continues to unsettle wealthy Westerners today. Some conclude that Jesus was talking about one of the city gates shaped like a needle, which was notoriously difficult for heavily laden camels to walk through. The sub-text of that is, 'With a bit of struggle and a slight tightening of our belts, we'll get through. He didn't really mean it to be *too* hard.' Whatever the correct interpretation of Jesus' imagery, it implies a radical change of lifestyle. A merchant would have to take everything off the camel's back for it to pass (albeit uncomfortably) through. The camel would have to scrape in, head bowed, and stripped of everything it 'owned'.

ACTION COUNTDOWN

> *'It's all too easy to distance ourselves from the dull implications of our daily financial transactions.'*
>
> Ethical Investors Group

- **Put a coin aside each day to save up and give away.**
  Accumulate loose coins, and give to charity foreign currency left over from holidays abroad.
- **Tithe.**
  Get into the habit of deducting a tenth of your income each pay-day to spend on God's work.
- **Take care with the remainder.**
  Your tithe's value is reduced if the lifestyle you choose exploits people and the earth.
- **Keep a week's tally of where your money goes.**
  Identify areas of waste and debt, and cut back so that your cash can be put to good use.

- **Use a credit card that gives to charity.**
  When you do resort to credit cards, ensure that you pick one where some of your money goes to deserving causes.
- **Send cash anonymously to someone you know needs help.**
  Become aware of gaps you could help fill among friends and neighbours.
- **Give away your interest.**
  Spend money you make on investments on someone else; and lend without charge too.
- **Live on a basic income and give the rest away, whatever you earn.**
  Like John Wesley, live *below* your means. Make out a will to leave money to your favourite cause too.
- **Have your church organize a 'Talent Contest'.**
  Like Jesus' parable of the talents, give members £5 that they must return with interest.
- **Organize a church LETS (Local Exchange Trading System) scheme.**
  Avoid cash, and share skills and possessions among the congregation. Extend the scheme into the surrounding community to help the unskilled, jobless, and those on low incomes.

MAKING CONTACT

Credit Action: *see* **G – GAMBLING.**

National Association of Citizens' Advice Bureaux:
  Check your phone book for details of your local branch.

National Debt Line: Monday and Thursday 10 a.m.–4 p.m., Tuesday and Wednesday 2 p.m.–7 p.m. Tel: 0121 359 8501. (Phone for free information pack dealing with debt.)

National Money Advice Association, 1st floor, Gresham House, 24 Holborn Viaduct, LONDON EC1A 2BN. Tel: 0171 236 3566.

Trading Standards Departments. (See under *Local Authority* in your phone book.)

Walletwatch: Tel: 0181 361 2411.

Negatives

'Do not worry about tomorrow, for tomorrow will worry about itself. Each day has enough trouble of its own.'

Jesus Christ

Introduction

It is very easy to become overwhelmed by the world's problems. Once you are aware of a social issue, and out of interest and concern choose to learn more, it will not be long before other broader issues demand your attention. The spread of AIDS, for example, touches upon issues of sexuality, drug abuse, morality, disability, provision of healthcare and housing, discrimination, Third World economics, and many other topics.

To show much concern can soon become overwhelming, and 'burn-out' is a recognized phenomenon among people who choose to give their all to help others. Fresh optimism can turn into cynicism and evolve into dark despair.

Christians are not immune from such negative feelings. There were times in Jesus' own ministry where hope seemed to vanish, when he felt forsaken by God, or was fearful and unsure of the bigger picture. Jesus' followers should take heart from this. All Jesus asks of us is that we first make the step of faith; strengthened by the knowledge of what God has done for us and growing in love for God, ourselves and the people around us, we do not need to *prove* our worth. We desire to do God's will; it is therefore fine to stand back and take a breather from our work without guilt. It is right too that we recognize the worth of the small action done for God. God does not ask us to save the world – that is *his* job.

> 'Whatever happens is God's will.'

It is easy for Christians to find themselves aligned with what might be termed the '*Que sera, sera*' tenet of the school of philosophy reflected in that old Doris Day song, since they believe in God's intervention in the world both historically and today. We can all cite examples of incidents that seemed more than mere coincidence (many Christians don't even believe in the concept), and places and situations to which we felt led. Yet God has given us free will and expects us to take responsibility for our actions. Often he will take us further than we ever imagined in our life plans, but, with our eyes on him, it is we who must make the first faltering step of faith in whatever we set out to do.

> 'Things haven't always been this bad.'

Nostalgia for 'the good ol' days' is a cosy way to absolve ourselves from any responsibility for today's culture ('in *my* day'), yet ignores the truth that the present is a consequence of the past, and that we are well and truly positioned in the now. The Bible itself declares that there is nothing new under the sun, and human behaviour is no worse or better than it ever was. Therefore to make-believe in some Golden Age when you could leave your front door open for the neighbours to pop in, and any breakdown in law and order was unheard of, is to ignore the truth that we mere mortals are of a fallen nature.

> 'Things *could* get worse.'

The history of civilizations is cyclical; they grow and evolve to the point where they are no longer sustainable and then implode. Also, the concept that human beings are somehow becoming better people over the centuries is not borne out by the facts. The twentieth-century cry of despair, 'How can we believe in God after the Holocaust?' is surely met by the response 'How can we believe in humanity?'

Suffering *does* occur and life as a Christian will not ensure immunity from life's woes. For many of history's people of faith, the exact opposite has been the case. Even in *today's* world, people are oppressed because they confess Jesus as their Lord. But although we must face darkness at some points in our lives, Jesus is by our side and we are thus never alone, and this pain will not outlast us. It is, then, possible to be an 'ultimate optimist', to believe that justice will one day be done even if not in our lifetime. That is the hope to which we can cling during times of trial, and to avoid cynicism and despair.

'What's the point?'

It's ironic that both those who believe in the spiritual realms (in God and an afterlife) *and* nihilists (who regard the material world that we see and know as all that there is), can reach the same point of wondering what life is *for*. The nihilist, seeing nothing beyond the grave, interprets life as ultimately futile. Christians too, seeing the *All* beyond the grave, can end up by interpreting actions in *this* world as ultimately futile – in other words, if everything's going to turn out all right in the end, if the story's going to have a happy ending anyway, why bother dealing with temporal earthly concerns? It's a classic example of our tendency to separate the spiritual from the physical, and to forget that our job on earth is living to glorify God, beginning his work of re-creation in the here-and-now by marking out territory so to speak, so that all might be made whole at the end of time.

ACTION COUNTDOWN

> *'Be still, and know that I am God.'*
>
> Psalm 46.10

- **Take time out.**
  Take a breather and allow yourself to unwind and play again.
- **Pray.**
  Spend time alone with God to recharge your batteries quietly and to realign your will with his.
- **Go easy on yourself.**
  Love yourself as much as you love God and your neighbours. Identify what makes you content, and treat yourself to something nice each day.
- **Always look on the bright side of life.**
  Count your blessings. Accentuate the positives and be thankful.
- **Just say no.**
  Our faith is not measured by the simple mass of our good works, but the quality of our hearts in the doing. Without love, our

actions are of little worth, so stop attempting to prove that you deserve God's grace, or striving to gain the approval of others. Simply love.

- **Go on retreat to a Christian community.**
  Ask your minister to suggest venues where you can spend time getting back on course.
- **Reappraise your lifestyle by living more simply.**
  Concentrate on what really matters to you and God. Why not cut down on the things you buy?
- **Find the point of your action.**
  Consider what you and others gain from any move you might make. Ask what you are doing.
- **Do something beautiful for God.**
  In God's eyes, one small step equals one giant leap. Why not hang out some nuts for the local birdlife?
- **Bear one another's burdens.**
  Reach out with a helping hand and lighten life's load for someone. Visit an elderly person who lives on his/her own.

ORGANIZATIONS

'No man is an island.'
John Donne

Introduction

The Christian Church has always been a *community* of saints, and this model of people uniting for a shared purpose has much to teach (and learn from) other organizations. This joining together of people of like mind on one issue draws together their differences also, and, ideally, individual strengths and weaknesses bond with those of others to produce a group of people who are individually, and en masse, the better for it. It is our value as individuals that God can put to good use in the company of others.

It is certainly tempting to go it alone in order to get things done, and arguably this is a temptation that is most strong among bright, independent women whose talents have been traditionally derided in the conventional Church and culture of their day. Yet such women – and similar types of men – are few in number. Certainly God needs and makes good use of visionaries who lead where others once feared treading – consider the work of Jackie Pullinger among drug addicts in Hong Kong, the social activist Sally Trench, and Florence Nightingale. Singular action can make a dramatic point. Jan Palach's 1968 suicide by fire as the Soviet tanks rolled into Prague stunned the world, and the image of the lone pro-democracy Chinese student in Tiananmen Square, carrier bag in hand, who walked directly up to a tank only for it to swerve time and again to avoid him, must be one of the most potent images of individual defiance and power recognized globally in recent times. Most people, though, are simply not made of such mettle. Certainly Christians by themselves can act as a force for good, but there is strength in numbers too. It is vital to have a vision, but it is far more powerful when it is shared among and grasped by others.

> 'But I can achieve more on my own.'

The voice of the masses is not always right, and so it is both right and honourable that any individual with an alternative viewpoint makes a stand for what he or she believes. In Nazi Germany, it was often the fringe-dwellers, like the shady lapsed Catholic businessman and womanizer Oskar Schindler, rather than the more 'respectable' and regular churchgoers, who chose not to turn a blind eye to the Holocaust. Yet Christians must also carefully ascertain whether what might be termed the 'Edward Scissorhands principle' – the gnawing temptation to go off and do your own thing when the general mood of opinion clashes with your own (as the strange scissorhanded character did in the film of the same name) – is a desire from God rather than self.

Certainly there are people whom God blesses in their solitude. The hermit, nun or monk's hours of aloneness – of prayer, study and thought – may, for all we know, be what keeps the world turning. Christianity is a community faith, though, that shares with and loves others. It is written in Genesis that it is not good for man to be alone. Therefore our moments of time alone with God must spur us to share with others what we know of Him.

> 'But to get anything done in a group, you have to go through a committee.'

Within most organizations, if you want to get involved at anything more than a surface level, you will experience basic bureaucracy. For the hands-on activist, this can be mind-numbingly dull. For the visionary, being confined by limitations can be incredibly frustrating. In order for organizations not to lose such valuable individuals, they must be given space to flourish. And the individuals concerned must prayerfully weigh up the pros and cons of staying put, or of taking their talents elsewhere.

> 'A leader's job is to take command.'

All too often, people in positions of power take too much control, so limiting the potential of those for whom they have responsibility. This occurs as much in church or Christian organizations as anywhere else.

Christ-like authority is different. Time and again in the Gospels, Jesus is seen to draw out the best from people; he sees what others have not perceived. Ultimately his position of leadership takes him to the cross and beyond, as he lays down his life and allows his followers to continue his work. Jesus has given us a pattern for leadership: the Christian is to be an enabler and encourager of honour and integrity. Their role is *team* leader, recognizing the gifts of each individual within their jurisdiction and giving them opportunity to use these gifts to their fullest potential while furthering the particular organization's aims. To that end, the Christian must be prepared to step down when someone in a junior position is ready for a more senior role. Christians who are not in leadership positions also have a vital role; with honesty and integrity, theirs must be a position of respect and loyalty to those in authority in order to work for the good of the organization in which they are involved.

> 'If it's not a Christian organization,
> it's not of God.'

The Christian Church has its own subcultures – its various leaders, its different books, its varieties of music, its prejudices – and so it is not surprising that many non-Christian activities are often frowned upon in some church circles. It is a brave Christian, then, who chooses to live and work among non-believers. But both the 1980s rise of the Green movement and the 1985 Live Aid concerts for Ethiopia proved that God does not only open the eyes of *Christians* to world needs. Everyone, whether believer or not, has something of God within them, and God will make use of that as he chooses.

ACTION COUNTDOWN

'Many hands make light work.'

- **List the organizations with which you are involved.**
  Consider what you already contribute to each.
- **Think what else you have to offer.**
  If you have time and energy to spare, work to contribute more of your talents.

- **List the organizations with which you would like to be involved.**
  Visit your public library to find out about local contacts of such groups – and get in touch.
- **Consider how organizations of similar concern might work together.**
  Many organizations have seen their cause forwarded when others have backed them.
- **Spread the word.**
  Any group needs new blood to keep it vibrant and contemporary, so invite friends along.
- **Get training and experience to further your cause.**
  Identify your strengths – whether they are communication, management, business, fundraising or campaigning skills – and make sure they are highly tuned.
- **Volunteer to take on a position of responsibility.**
  Get more involved as a secretary, treasurer, press officer, or president.
- **Obtain employment in your field of interest.**
  Submit your curriculum vitae to bodies for whom you would like to work.
- **Identify an area of need that is not being met.**
  Canvass other organizations on how a new group might meet clear needs and avoid overlap.
- **Start up a new group.**
  Spread your vision by inspiring others to work towards a common purpose. Aim to work yourself and volunteers out of a job by campaigning for an achievable goal!

POVERTY

'The spirit of the Lord is upon me, because he has anointed me to preach the good news to the poor. He has sent me to heal the brokenhearted, to proclaim liberty to the captives, and recovery of sight to the blind, to set at liberty those who are oppressed, to proclaim the acceptable year of the Lord.'

Jesus Christ

Facts of the matter

- More than 70 per cent of those who live in poverty throughout the world are women.
- Every 35 seconds, a child is born into poverty in the USA.
- According to British government figures, 1 in 4 (13.7 million) people (including children) were living in poverty in 1993–5 compared with 1 in 10 in 1979.
- There is no official UK 'poverty line'. Government, and groups like the Child Poverty Action Group, set 'low income status' at the level of income support, or 50 per cent of the nation's average income after housing costs: £65 for a single adult, £118 for a couple, £196 for a couple with 3 children under 12, and £118 for all family types.
- Some 32 per cent of UK households don't own a car. Some 51 per cent of British women have no driving licence.
- The unemployed are at greatest risk of poverty, but poverty in work is on the rise: 12 per cent of the nation's employees now live in poverty, a steep rise from 4 per cent in 1979.[1]
- Around 58 per cent of single parents live in poverty, but couples with children are the largest group.
- Approximately 26 per cent of pensioner couples, and 35 per cent of single pensioners, live in poverty.
- According to government figures, 750,000 pensioners who should be on income support, and 400,000 who should be on housing benefit, are not. They either do not understand

how to claim benefits or war pensions, or are unaware that they are eligible for them.

- The official designation of living in 'overcrowded conditions' is over 1.5 people per room.
- One-third of people begging have a substance abuse problem. Drink or drugs help to block out despair, but add to bad diet and health problems, and can prevent people from finding a solution.[2]

Introduction

Poverty in the UK is often well hidden. Apart from coming across the occasional *Big Issue* vendor during the journey from suburban home via commuter train to the office, there is often little chance of meeting any of the one in four of the population who live in poverty.

Yet statistics from organizations like the Joseph Rowntree Foundation paint a very different and scary image of life in the UK. Social service provision is diminishing, so those on low income are without help; many people cannot even afford basic dental treatment. A two-tier society has emerged. There are the moneyed majority with relative choice to buy housing, insurance, education and medical care, and there are the third of all UK households that are dependent on state aid.

Writer James Baldwin pointed out 35 years ago: 'Anyone who has ever struggled with poverty knows how extremely expensive it is to be poor; if one is a member of a captive population, economically speaking, one's feet are on a treadmill forever. One is victimized, economically, in a thousand ways – via rent, or car insurance.' For example, the rich benefit from tax cuts that are unavailable to the poor. Homeowners receive mortgage benefits, while those who rent properties receive no rebate. Additionally, benefits are increasingly tightened: housing benefit is now related to the market price of property in a given area rather than the set price for any individual property. Those on social security must pay the difference from their already low income. Those with access to their own transport shop at out-of-town supermarkets, thus depriving local traders – and the people dependent on them, such as pensioners, those with disabilities, and mothers with small children. The consequence is that local prices soar while the large out-of-town supermarkets are able to keep food prices low.

In our day-to-day lives, we may have little contact with the poor. However, they *are* in our midst, and as Christians knowing this we have a moral duty to work for their benefit.

> 'People don't know what poverty is. In the 1930s, children had no shoes.'

The gap between Britain's wealthy and its poor has not been so great since the 1930s, yet that was at a time when the social services we have today were simply not in existence. Today, mass production methods and the quick-turnover consumer culture have made cheap or second-hand goods available to the poor.

Yet even people with experience of working among the poor of the Third World have been appalled at the conditions within certain parts of the UK's inner cities. There are still many families who are hopelessly locked in poverty, and people on income support or limited incomes who are unable to afford dental treatment or glasses. Tuberculosis, an illness to which those in poor and overcrowded housing are particularly susceptible, is on the rise again, and asthma levels are soaring.

> 'It's those single mothers who are to blame.'

Young women with children, but no partner, have been made a scapegoat for many of society's ills. They're seen to jump the housing queues, and are generally regarded as the undeserving poor. Their own children are seen as the next generation of welfare state dependants, so many taxpayers would be happy to see their benefits cut. This attitude, while ignoring statistical evidence indicating that most single mothers are divorcees in their thirties (and many of them from *middle-class* backgrounds), gives little hope to people trapped in poverty, and promotes the idea of a detached and threatening inner-city underclass.

> 'The poor can grow their own food
> on allotments.'

When government ministers make such declarations, what they actually *do* mean is 'let them eat potatoes'. Research indicates that people's eating habits are clearly linked to how much they earn. Better-off households buy more fruit (but less bread) per person than poorer households. As income increases, the amount of carbohydrate per head consumed decreases. While home-grown food can certainly supplement a diet, the belief that Britons are a nation of market gardeners is rather out of touch. Many inner-city allotments proved ripe for development during the 1980s property boom; and a culture geared to 'fast food' (whether that is takeaway burgers, or oven-ready supermarket meals), means that people are less used to growing their own and making do with less.

> 'A bit of hardship didn't stop me from getting
> where I am today.'

The American dream of the individual at the bottom of the pile being able to pull themselves up by their own bootstraps and make something big of their lives is a myth that is attractive to people in the UK too. The theory goes that if you are hardworking enough, whatever your original circumstances, you will make it to the top one day. Yet, for every person who does, there are plenty who remain where they started. Limited education, employment, healthcare and environment easily stifle potential, and it takes a strong will and singlemindedness to break out beyond such circumstances.

'Poverty is at the root of powerlessness ... poor people are trapped in housing and in environments over which they have little control. They lack the means and opportunity, which so many of us take for granted, of making choices in their lives.'

Faith in the City, the Archbishop of Canterbury's
Report on Urban Priority Areas, 1985

ACTION COUNTDOWN

'The Church's role is to point up areas of need which haven't been spotted by the mainstream of society. It shows that something can be done. It's in the same tradition as when churches began hospitals and schools in the past – providing until the State picked up the idea.'

The Reverend Paul Regan, who set up a drop-in centre in east London for people in Bed & Breakfast accommodation

- **Invite friends on a low income around for a meal.**
  Or make sure you visit them – and be sure to treat them sensitively, not as charity cases.
- **Become familiar with the benefits system.**
  Pick up leaflets from your Post Office to discover what is available to people on low incomes.
- **Become a Citizens' Advice Bureau volunteer.**
  See *Yellow Pages* for your local branch, and serve the growing numbers dependent on the Citizens' Advice Bureaux.
- **Start up a food co-op among friends and neighbours, and let it grow.**
  Buy in bulk from suppliers, and establish a local low-price community distribution service.
- **Provide a nappy cleaning service.**
  Set up a rota system among friends with time and good washing-machines to help local families choose a cheap and environmentally friendly alternative to disposables.
- **Establish a furniture exchange.**
  Ask your council for a collection point so that unwanted furniture can be redistributed.
- **Conduct a local community survey on behalf of your church.**
  Unite with local churches, social services, GPs and police to profile your area.
- **Provide a help service.**
  Use your research findings to best serve local people's needs in a practical way.
- **Set up a debt advice service at your church.**
  Provide a financial lifeline for people trapped in debt.

- **Set up a community bank that provides loans at low interest.**
  Help people to escape the trap of loan sharks and pawn shops, and so get back up on their feet.

MAKING CONTACT

Age Concern: *see* **D – DISABILITY.**

Child Poverty Action Group: *see* **C – CHILDREN.**

Church Urban Fund, 2 Great Peter Street, LONDON SW1P 3LX. Tel: 0171 620 0917/8.

Evangelical Coalition for Urban Mission, Frontier Centre, 70–74 City Road, LONDON EC1Y 2BJ. Tel: 0171 336 7744.

Family Welfare Association, 501–505 Kingsland Road, LONDON E8 4AU. Tel: 0171 254 6251.

Institute for Fiscal Studies, 7 Ridgmount Street, LONDON WC1E 7AE. Tel: 0171 636 3784.

Joseph Rowntree Foundation, The Homestead, 40 Water End, YORK YO3 6LP. Tel: 01904 629241.

Low Pay Unit, 27–29 Amwell Street, LONDON EC1R 1UN. Tel: 0171 713 7616.

National Council on Ageing: *see* **Age Concern.**

UK Action, Tear Fund, 100 Church Road, TEDDINGTON, Middlesex TW11 8QE. Tel: 0181 977 9144.

'When I give food to the poor, they call me a saint. When I ask why the poor have no food, they call me a communist.'

Dom Helder Camara

QUESTIONS

'I am a spiritual director; my experience in ministry is chiefly that of listening to what happens to people when they pray, when they recognize God in their lives. And in this work I am repeatedly reminded that questions and doubts can be an essential part of the movement towards change and growth.'

Pia Buxton of the Roman Catholic Order,
the Institute of the Blessed Virgin Mary

Introduction

While there are strong intellectual reasons to believe in God, the Christian life must begin with a step of faith, a moment of sheer *belief* when one must risk entering unknown territory. But it is not unusual for Christians to remain at that 'just over the threshold' stage, afraid of any questioning that could shake their faith to its core, and lead them away from God.

Christianity is a living faith, not a stagnant one. Life's spiritual path does not, and must not, remain at the point of simply *recognizing* who Jesus is. There are always new questions to ask. For in the same way that individuals evolve and develop on emotional, physical and mental levels, so too does our understanding of what it means to be a Christian. In the same way that monochrome adolescent idealism gives way to the broad spectrum of adult viewpoints, the absolute certainty of the new convert should eventually shift to a more muted way of looking at the world in the light of a deep and long-term relationship with God. Christianity is about offering our whole self – mind, body and spirit – to God, following him with our emotional instincts *and* our brains in gear. This way, we can truly make an impact in a world clearly unsure of where it is heading.

> 'Christianity has all the answers.'

Living in a highly rational world that constantly seeks answers puts a lot of pressure on Christians. Honesty about our uncertainty, though, can say as much to people: 'I don't know everything, I can't know everything, but I still have faith.' Paul declares that for today 'we see but through a glass darkly', yet we know we have encountered God and that our lives are transformed by that.

> 'Once you're a Christian, you don't need to think.'

Christians must question, think and doubt in order to have a truly genuine explanation of what they believe. That does not come from blind faith, but rather from a tackling of subjects encountered in our daily lives as citizens of planet Earth in the late twentieth century.

> 'Being a Christian is purely about saving souls.'

Christianity is an evangelistic faith, letting people know the good news of Jesus Christ. However, if new Christians in their turn see Christianity purely in those terms, and so introduce someone to Christ to do likewise, few will grasp the true magnitude of what it means to follow Jesus.

Jesus taught that the two most important Commandments are to love the Lord your God with all your heart, and to love your neighbour as yourself. To love God, to love your neighbour, and to love yourself, are all major tasks that should inspire our every action, however small. Those actions will produce a knock-on effect, rippling out into our society and across the world. Such is our task, and it is one fuelled by God's infinite love for us.

> 'If you start asking questions, you'll never stop. You'll intellectualize God out of existence.'

In the same way that God is big enough to take our anger and frustration of what life throws at us, he is there for our doubts too. If we keep our eyes on him, then our questions about life and faith, and any confusion we may have, are kept in their proper place. God becomes the central focus of our lives and, bathed in that awesome Light, our questions, fears and doubts are seen from their true perspective.

> 'There are clear Christian standpoints on most issues. If you don't hold those views, then you can't be a Christian.'

Certainly Christian tradition coupled with accepted biblical interpretation places strong emphasis on ways of living. The sense that other Christians have battled through life with their hand in God's hand is a source of strength to many believers. However, it disregards God's ongoing revelation to his flock through history. For example, until the last century, being pro-slavery was regarded as entirely consistent with being a Christian, yet Christians in this country initiated the global anti-slavery movement.

Additionally, there are many inconsistencies in so-called Christian viewpoints that reflect social class rather than faith. For some believers, gambling on the National Lottery or football pools is out, but investing in shares is acceptable. Or being in debt is frowned upon unless, of course, one has a mortgage. Abortion is abhorrent, but the 'right to life' of death-row criminals is denied. As Christians, we must be constantly on our guard, testing our opinions and ready to change them as God reveals more of himself to each one of us.

ACTION COUNTDOWN

> 'Ask and it will be given to you; seek and you will find; knock and the door will be opened to you. For everyone who asks receives; he who seeks finds; and to him who knocks, the door will be opened.'
>
> Jesus Christ

- **Read a book from a modern translation of the New Testament each day.**
  Try to read the *New International Version* or the *Good News*

Bible like a novel, in order to grasp an overall sense of Jesus' mission.

- **Read a newspaper that conflicts with your political views.**
  Read it impartially, and consider the validity of the alternative opinions it holds.
- **Use newspaper stories to inform your prayer life.**
  Ask yourself and God about the Christian perspective on different topics – and whether there is one.
- **Read Christian books that put both sides of the argument.**
  Let your mind be stretched by the differing views that fellow Christians hold.
- **Listen to what people have to say.**
  Often we are too ready to spout our own opinions, but we learn much by remaining silent. Trust and friendship can deepen as people gain space to be open and honest with each other.
- **Ask questions.**
  Be prepared to offer your own opinion and ask questions with grace and humility.
- **Start a church debating group in your home.**
  Decide on a topic (homelessness, the NHS, relationships) in advance in order to keep debate informed.
- **Join a pressure group or political party that reflects your views.**
  Allow your Christian faith to colour, and be coloured by, the world around you.
- **Let actions speak louder than words.**
  The test of your Christian faith and political views is in the life choices you make.
- **Gather together like-minded friends.**
  Support each other in making practical differences to the communities in which you live.

MAKING CONTACT

Christian Ecology Link: *see* **E – ENVIRONMENT.**

Christian Impact: *see* **K – KINGDOM.**

Christian Socialist Movement, 36 Old Queen Street, LONDON SW1H 9JF. Tel: 0171 976 7881.

Conservative and Unionist Party, Central Office, 32 Smith Square, LONDON SW1P 3HH. Tel: 0171 222 9000.

Evangelical Alliance: *see* **K – KINGDOM.**

Green Party, 1A Waterlow Road, LONDON N19 5NJ.
Tel: 0171 272 4474.

Labour Party, John Smith House, 150 Walworth Road, LONDON
SE17 1JT. Tel: 0171 701 1234.

Liberal Democrats, 4 Cowley Street, LONDON SW1P 3NB.
Tel: 0171 222 7999.

Northern Ireland Green Party, 537 Antrim Road, BELFAST
BT15 3BU. Tel: 01232 776731.

Plaid Cymru, 51 Cathedral Road, CARDIFF CF1 9HD.
Tel: 01222 231944.

Plaid Werdd Cymru/Wales Green Party, 38 Queen Street,
ABERYSTWYTH, Dyfed, Wales SY23 1PU. Tel: 01970 611226.

Scottish Conservative and Unionist Party, Central Office,
Suite 1/1, 14 Links Place, Leith, EDINBURGH EH6 7EZ.
Tel: 0131 555 2900.

Scottish Green Party, 11 Greenbank Terrace, EDINBURGH
EH10 6ER. Tel: 0131 447 1843.

Scottish Liberal Democrats, 4 Clifton Terrace, EDINBURGH
EH12 5DR. Tel: 0131 337 2314.

Scottish National Party, 6 North Charlotte Street, EDINBURGH
EH2 4JH. Tel: 0131 226 3661.

Social Democrats and Labour Party (Northern Ireland),
Cranmore House, 6110 Lisburn Road, BELFAST BT9 7GT.
Tel: 01232 668100.

Ulster Democratic Unionist Party, 3 Glengall Street, BELFAST
BT12 5AE. Tel: 01232 324601.

Welsh Liberal Democrats, 57 St Mary Street, CARDIFF CF1 1FE.
Tel: 01222 382210.

RIGHTS

'Rights are what must be achieved if there is to be any element of justice in society, particularly the right to life, liberty and equality before the law. Ideals tell what might be achieved in a society where there is perfect justice. Goals and objectives indicate what are considered to be realistic aims.'

Philip Crowe, in *A Whisper Will Be Heard* (Fount, 1994)

Facts of the matter

- Since its beginning in 1961, Amnesty International and its supporters have campaigned on behalf of 43,500 'Prisoners of Conscience'. Of these cases, 40,000 are now closed.
- Though banned under international law, one-third of the world still uses torture to oppress its populace.[1]
- Over 630 million more people embrace democracy today than in 1986.
- There are 300 million tribal people world-wide, yet their lives, lands and human rights remain relentlessly persecuted.[2]
- Since 1989, over £32 million of British overseas aid has been directed towards police training in countries such as Indonesia and Nigeria.[3]
- Only one-fifth of Britain's 1.5 million acres of Britain's common land allows public access rights.[4]
- Of 43 local authorities that took part in the Maternity Alliance's 1990 survey on travelling families, 16 said they would evict pregnant women, 13 would evict pregnant women close to birth, and 15 would evict mothers with a newborn baby.[5]
- The UK's prison population is the highest in Europe.

Introduction

Throughout the world, the Universal Declaration of Human

Rights, originally agreed by the United Nations in 1948, is the most widely accepted affirmation of the rights of people. However, there has been long-running debate over what a human right actually *is*.

In the West, human rights have been synonymous with multi-party elections, freedom of speech and assembly, while in the former Soviet Union, they meant having enough to eat, a place to live, decent healthcare, and education. Human rights are interdependent, as was recognized when civil and political, economic, social and cultural rights were given equal status in international human rights treatises after the Second World War.

Citizens' rights have evolved since 1948, placing the individual first – and putting governments under greater pressure to bestow rights. Across the world, aid donors increasingly make their benefits conditional on governments improving human rights records, fuelling the global spread of multi-party democracy. Yet despite such groundbreaking moves throughout the world – and in our own nation – rights enshrined in international law continue to be flouted.

In the UK today, injustice is promoted via some of our laws and systems. People seeking asylum are imprisoned as they await administration procedure, a procedure that Amnesty International strongly opposes. The repeal of the Caravan Sites Act meant that local authority duty to gypsies would not include new travellers, now in effect living legally only when their vehicles are on the move. Under the Criminal Justice Act, police were given the right to stop and search individuals even if there be no grounds to suspect them of doing anything wrong. Also, people now have no right to remain silent once they are arrested, so can be pressurized into making false confessions.

Humanity and its laws are imperfect, and because power changes hands and is never permanent, it is vital to remain ever vigilant that justice is carried out.

> 'If people are good law-abiding citizens, they have nothing to fear.'

The oft-quoted scientific research revealing that a frog kept in water gradually heated to boiling point does nothing to escape, while one dropped in boiling water will immediately leap out, relates to how we view society and its changing values. Often it is not until we, and those we know, are directly affected by loss of rights that we take notice. As Christians, we must be ready to take a stand before a situation deteriorates to that extent. Security measures, such as the introduction of closed-circuit television to control crime, can in other circumstances be used to monitor the lives of ordinary citizens too. Universal identity cards would have very different uses under a dictatorship.

In Nazi Germany, it was often the people on the fringes of society who were most aware, and most vocal, about the downside of fascism. Laws are not always in keeping with God's laws and, as Christians, our duty is not keeping a low profile as respectable members of society, but honouring God in all that we say and do.

> 'But we live in a democracy.'

Although technically there is a system of 'one man, one vote' in the UK, the two main political parties seem interested only in targeting 'middle England'. Other groups are statistically less likely to vote and, ironically, the less their viewpoint is respected, the less it is worth their while to do so. Parliament ends up representing the 'haves', while anyone else's voice remains largely unheard.

Even if a broader cross-section of lifestyles and viewpoints were heeded and a higher percentage of people chose to vote, without proportional representation the British 'first past the post' election system remains in essence undemocratic. Political parties need a minimum of £500 to put up a single candidate, so more value is placed on the size of a group's wallet than the worth of its views. The House of Lords remains largely a body of people elevated to power because their ancestors received favours for services rendered to past monarchs. There are also a growing number of official unelected quangos with nationwide power, plus private police and security groups effectively taking the law into their own hands.

> 'Regardless of anyone else, I have the right to
> determine my own life.'

'No man is an island', said poet John Donne. Our lifestyle choices affect how our neighbours live too. Rights must recognize responsibilities, and not infringe the rights of others. Those who take their own life, for example, will affect the lives of everyone else, leaving a gap by their absence. To give up your life – unless you are laying it down so another might live – can threaten the lives of all. Voluntary euthanasia by an individual in fact devalues the lives of others, by threatening anyone who is deemed to have a 'poor quality of life': the elderly, terminally ill, mentally disabled, criminals etc.

> 'Rights are made in the minds of
> men and women.'

Since the whole concept of rights is created by men and women, it is ultimately valueless. One individual's right equals another's oppression, and there is no higher authority to which we can turn to establish law. The concept of what is right and wrong is thus relative; any action, however evil, can be justified since there is no higher Truth to set it against. Amid such chaos, the honesty and integrity of Christians should shine forth by offering some sense of stability and order, with love at its core.

ACTION COUNTDOWN

'You support us because you believe in the right to freedom. The right to live without fear and terror. The right to defend yourself against tyranny and injustice. The right to respect, dignity and fair treatment.'

Amnesty International

- **Listen to the singer Sting's** 'They dance' **and** 'How fragile we are', **songs respectively about the 'disappeared' of Chile, and the frailty of human life, from Sting's album entitled** *Nothing Like the Sun.*

Jot down your thoughts and feelings, and use this as a basis for prayer.

- **Use the United Nations' Universal Declaration of Human Rights during Bible study.**
  Either individually or with others, consider each Article in the context of your faith. Is it being met here or abroad? What action can we take to promote human rights?

- **Consider your own and others' responses to what people say or do.**
  Are they aggressive, passive or manipulative? Are others given space to be themselves?

- **Do a course in assertiveness training.**
  Many Christians fall into the trap of thinking God wants them for a doormat. He does not.

- **Aim to live a life of faith, honour and integrity.**
  Stand tall and strong by being true to God, yourself, and those around you.

- **Read Terry Waite's, Brian Keenan's and John McCarthy's/ Jill Morrell's books about being held in captivity.**
  Consider the different perspectives on being held in a Beirut gaol. How would *you* feel?

- **Join Amnesty International.**
  Raise a voice on behalf of those world-wide whom others try to silence.

- **Train to be a volunteer for the Citizens' Advice Bureaux (CAB).**
  CAB is literally a godsend for many in times of hardship and exploitation.

- **Train to be a solicitor or lawyer.**
  Serve people in a legal capacity, such as representing people on the USA's Death Row.

- **Set up a legal advice centre.**
  Use your church as a community base from which justice can be done for those without help.

MAKING CONTACT

Amnesty International: *see* **L – LETTERS.**

Charter 88: *see* **J – JUSTICE.**

Christian Solidarity International, PO Box 99, NEW MALDEN, Surrey KT3 3YF. Tel: 0181 942 8810.

Jubilee Campaign: *see* **C – CHILDREN.**

Medical Foundation for the Care of Victims of Torture, 96–8 Grafton Road, LONDON NW5 3EJ. Tel: 0171 813 7777.

Minority Rights Group, 379 Brixton Road, LONDON SW9 7DE. Tel: 0171 978 9498.

National Council for Civil Liberties: *see* **J – JUSTICE.**

Ramblers Association (RA): *see* **E – ENVIRONMENT.**

Survival International, 11–15 Emerald Street, LONDON WC1N 3QL. Tel: 0171 242 1441.

SOCIETY

*'Love the Lord God with all your heart and all your soul, and
love your neighbour as yourself.'*

Jesus Christ

Introduction

Many people feel that Britain is no longer a Christian country.
Cultural trends seem to bear this out – the introduction of the
National Lottery is but one example. Yet even the most strident
of humanist, atheist or non-Christian religious people cannot deny
that Christianity's hold on British culture has been, and remains,
strong. Most British people at times of deep desperation will pray
to the Christian God they recall from childhood teachings, even
if they never now attend church. The very social structures that
form the pillars of our cultural environment were established on
Christian lines. The history of social reform, law or of art in
Britain is intrinsically Christian, and that cannot and should not
be denied.

The challenge for today's Christians is to regain a strong social
vision where it has been lost, and so provide real hope for the
future. Many valuable institutions – such as those concerned with
health and education – improved the lives of this nation's people
in years gone by and are now being eroded. In areas of art, music,
literature and film, the Christian voice often seems incredibly quiet
when it should be making a response to an oft-peddled bland
nihilism. And as almost half of all UK marriages fragment, the
Church must help pick up the pieces and restore the victims of
broken relationships. Jesus pointed out that the most important
of the Ten Commandments were the first two; and that out of
keeping those, the other eight were, by definition, kept. Social
order is obtained via our love for God, for the people around us,
and for ourselves.

> 'There is no such thing as society.'

This bold 1980s statement by Margaret Thatcher, the then Prime Minister, has left its mark; and in a money-oriented society it was exactly what so many of those who had prospered financially wanted to hear. Gone was any sense of responsibility, any sense that from those who had much, much would be expected. Victorian philanthropists such as the library-funding Carnegie, the Quaker families of Fry and Rowntree, and Shaftesbury and Barnardo who used their money for the civic good, were quietly forgotten, and free-market individualism was ruthlessly promoted. When many who 'bought into' the 1980s creed were hit by redundancies, negative equity or repossession in the recession-hit 1990s, Mrs Thatcher's words left a sour taste. If there was no society, who was there to help you when things went wrong?

> 'It's between me and God.'

Pressure to conform to a particular perception of what it means to be Christian can leave individuals resentful and defensive about their faith. For others, it is when life buffets them from all sides, and all 'religion' is stripped away, that all they can do is hold on to the truth that God *is*. So there is some place for this one-to-one communion, yet Christianity is ultimately based on relationship and *community*. The love of God expresses itself in working together and loving others. Because of this, the Church can be viewed as a true model for action. At its best, it has a conscience about what is wrong with the world and offers hope, provides strength in numbers, and reaches out to those who are suffering.

> 'Non-Christians are not my concern.'

It is incredibly easy for Christians to isolate themselves from non-believers. Fellowship groups, church meetings and conferences often take up an incredible amount of time, and can prevent individuals from making real contact with people who have most need of knowing God. Many Christians grow unaccustomed too to any activity that is more than an opportunity to 'bring someone to Christ'. In such a climate, many non-believers grow suspicious of our invitations and the opportunity to develop genuine relationships based on unconditional love is lost.

> 'I am not my brother's keeper.'

Cain's words to God, hiding the fact that he had murdered his brother Abel, echo down through history. Many of us choose to turn a blind eye to others' suffering. 'If we can take care of ourselves, then why can't they?' we say to ourselves. Yet in any community there will always be a percentage of people who, for whatever reason, cannot manage on their own. Christ requests that we reveal his love and compassion in practical ways to anyone in need.

It has been calculated that there are six degrees of separation between each one of us and community with the whole world. Like a web, the contacts we have with others spread out to touch strangers across the world. The Jewish saying 'he who saves the life of one man saves the whole world' therefore makes real sense. We are not far removed, then, from our neighbour; he or she inhabits the same world. What happens to them could so easily happen to us – in other words, there, but for the grace of God, go I.

ACTION COUNTDOWN

'When I needed a neighbour, were you there?'

- **Work your way through your address book.**
  Renew friendships by phone or post, and also arrange to meet up if possible.
- **Extend your friendships.**
  Show how much you care by appropriate gifts, visits and remembering special days.
- **Be an anonymous benefactor.**
  Reach out to those around you through gifts and help without identifying yourself.
- **Get to know your neighbours.**
  Introduce yourself to people at home and work, and aim to be someone to whom they can turn.

- **Invite people to church and social activities.**
  And make it a two-way relationship by accepting their invitations.
- **Mix and match the people you know.**
  Break down barriers by introducing people from different areas of your life to one another.
- **Pray as if you were a pebble in a pond sending out ripples.**
  From people close to you, to acquaintances, communities, governments, countries, the world . . .
- **Consider other practical ways you can improve matters.**
  Think about the people, places and issues that God brings to your mind and how you can help.
- **Use leaflets to keep people informed about a world of need.**
  It is perfectly legal to hand out leaflets to passers-by, though shop doorways and the pavement must not be obstructed. Or put up a noticeboard in your front garden.
- **Follow Jesus' guidelines.**
  Use Matthew 25.34–40 as a step-by-step basis for action to reach out to the world.

THIRD WORLD

'There is enough for every man's need. Not every man's greed.'
Mahatma Gandhi

Facts of the matter

- Malnutrition affects one-fifth of the world's population – about a billion people. Some 80,000 people die of hunger and disease in the Third World every day, 44,000 of them children.
- Half of the population of the Third World are under 19 years old.
- Approximately 79 per cent of Britons want the UK overseas aid budget to stay the same or be increased.
- Of 42 sub-Saharan countries awarded British aid in 1993, 10 received private funds from the UK as opposed to British government support.[1]
- The UK spends less than the UN target of at least 0.15 per cent of GNP on Third World aid.[2]
- Tax relief to British banks on provisions for Third World debts amounts to $7 billion – over 3 times Britain's annual aid to the Third World.
- Sales of the world's 4 largest companies exceed Africa's entire GNP.
- About 75 per cent of employees of the huge, transnational toy companies are from Asia.[3]
- Globally, poor countries with big arms budgets get twice as much aid per person as those that spend less on military goods.
- In 1992, Pakistan ordered 40 Mirage 2000E fighters and 3 Tripartite aircraft from France. The cost of the deal equalled 2 years of safe water for 55 million people, family planning services for all 20 million couples, essential medicines for the

13 million without healthcare, and basic education for 12 million children.[4]

- Globally, 40,000 companies control 70 per cent of world trade. Some 90 per cent of these companies are based in the West, but their products are made where costs are lowest. In 1965–85, US multinationals took an average £377 million more each year out of independent African states than they put in.[5]
- Manhattan has more telephone lines than the whole of sub-Saharan Africa.[6]

Introduction

The everyday way we live in the West affects the way people live in the most destitute parts of the world. Our lifestyle is maintained by keeping two-thirds of the world in poverty. For produce to be kept at a relatively affordable price in our shops, cheap labour will be bought in the Third World, tariffs on imported goods kept high, and the lowest possible price paid for cash crops that we cannot grow ourselves – such as exotic fruits and coffee and cocoa.

The resulting global economic patterns involve infant-aged children as well as adults working in factories where the health and safety conditions of developed countries don't apply, obstacles placed on Third World goods entering the West, and people being forced to live on dangerous floodplains and perched on hillsides as the best land is cultivated to feed Western mouths. The burden of people in the Third World is made harder by the global arms trade. Most people struggling to live in developing countries are unaware that their government's spending on military and foreign arms far outweighs the money invested in, say, food and healthcare.

Yet it is not only the people of the Third World who are affected by their impoverished state. Keeping the Third World poor – while in the short term a cheap option in terms of labour and raw materials for multinational companies and ourselves – is ultimately bad for business. Instead of encouraging an open market where development, growth and trade can flourish, and employment and income is generated both here and abroad, the rich resources of the Third World are trapped in paying off the interest of debts to Western banks, or devalued via limiting tariffs and quotas imposed by the West. The concept of a global competitive free market is a myth, for the Third World is debarred from it.

> 'There are too many people.'

While the world's population is increasing rapidly, it is pressure on the world's resources rather than sheer numbers that creates need. The lifestyle of each Westerner is far more destructive than an entire Third World family unit.

People in the Third World have large families for a range of reasons. The most pressing need in countries with minimal social services or healthcare provision is for a workforce who will continue to help out when parents are too old to look after themselves. Also, when child mortality is high, large families ensure that at least some will reach adulthood. The stories of our own families reveal this principle: for as living and educational standards increase, family size tends to reduce.

> 'Without our help, the Third World wouldn't stand a chance.'

It is tempting to believe that before the dawn of the British Empire, the world beyond our shores was in darkness, waiting for our civilizing process. Yet the historical, biblical and archaeological evidence belies this perspective. Before the UK's Industrial Revolution of the nineteenth century, African and Asian nations had produced great civilizations. And while the world's railway systems owe much to British invention, we made sure that we benefited economically from everything we gave. In other words, the concept of the Commonwealth is primarily for our own island's benefit.

Even when we do give altruistically – as during 1985's Live Aid frenzy – what our nation claws back in the way of tariffs on Third World produce is ten times the value – which, in effect, all but cancels out a mass act of love. Additionally, Third World wars are waged with Western weapons that our politicians and banks are happy to sanction; aid is given in exchange for arms contracts, prolonging wars that devastate and destabilize nations.

> 'A child will die tonight if you don't give . . .'

Many charities go for the 'emotional jugular' when collecting or campaigning on behalf of people in the Third World. However, it can create the exact opposite effect. So-called 'compassion fatigue' is very much related to an overwhelming sense of impotence: that whatever one may do will not make an iota of difference; that child will be dead by the time my money gets to Africa.

It was Michael Buerk's measured tones on the television news that prompted Bob Geldof to establish Band Aid, realizing that a manmade problem could be solved largely by the good of people. He recognized that he had a duty to be a force for good. Additionally, we need to understand that Third World poverty is very much linked to the way that the West chooses to live – and that as consumers we have the tremendous power of choice to support global fair trade.

> 'Tariffs and quotas on Third World imports
> protect UK employees' jobs.'

In the UK, it has been more often automation and rationalization that have forced people out of work rather than barriers placed on people beyond our shores; and keeping prices of labour and resources down overseas, by default devalues the worth of our own. To compete, UK employees are encouraged to accept fewer rights and security of work. The obsession of the world's powers with economic growth – and the systems put in place to promote it – have to be challenged, and alternative ways of living sought if the world order is to be more just.

'Fairer shares in the family of mankind will begin to happen when the prices of goods go up in our shops and wages are not lifted to match them. Quite simply, there is no other way. This society of excessive consumption exists within, and indeed thrives upon, a larger society of excessive need. This is the context of our plenty, and our plenty is not making things better, but worse . . .'

Michael Taylor, Director of Christian Aid.

'Suppose a brother or sister is without clothes and daily food. If one of you says to him, "Go, I wish you well; keep warm and well fed," but does nothing about his physical needs, what good is it? In the same way, faith by itself, if it is not accompanied by action, is dead.'

James 2.15–17

- **Give and take from your local Oxfam store.**
  Deposit your own unwanted goods there, and buy secondhand and fairly traded goods too.
- **Buy fairly traded goods.**
  The Fair Trade Foundation logo reveals products that do not harm people or the environment.
- **Make simple clothes and blankets for people overseas.**
  Oxfam need people to knit or sew up blanket squares and make children's dresses and shorts.
- **Collect money for Christian Aid during their annual fundraising week.**
  Or if you run a youth group, sign up for World Vision's annual 24-hour famine in March.
- **Campaign on behalf of the Third World.**
  Don't just rattle a tin – join your local group of World Development Movement activists to improve people's lives.
- **Campaign to get fairly traded goods into your local supermarket.**
  Around five people in a week, locally requesting certain products, will alert a Head Office.
- **Sponsor a child or elderly person in the Third World.**
  Support an individual *and* their community via Tear Fund, Action Aid or Help the Aged.
- **Start a prayer group for the world.**
  Register with Tear Fund's World Watch Prayer Link to stay informed of countries in need.
- **Be a church representative to sell Tearcraft or Traidcraft goods.**
  Ensure that post-worship coffee is fairly traded too.
- **Use your skills overseas.**
  Serve Third World communities, either long or short term, via established organizations.

MAKING CONTACT

CAFOD, Romero Close, Stockwell Road, LONDON SW9 9TY.
Tel: 0171 733 7900.

Christian Aid, PO Box 100, LONDON SE1 7RT. Tel: 0171 620 4444.

Earthscan: *see* **E – ENVIRONMENT.**

Intermediate Technology Development Group, Myson House,
Railway Terrace, RUGBY, Warwickshire CV21 3HT.
Tel: 01788 560631.

International Voluntary Service: *see* **K – KINGDOM.**

Mission Aviation Fellowship, Ingles Manor, Castle Hill Avenue,
FOLKESTONE, Kent CTO 2TN. Tel: 01303 850950.

Out Of This World, 52 Elswick Road, NEWCASTLE UPON TYNE
NE4 6JH. Tel: 0191 272 1601.

Overseas Development Administration (ODA), 94 Victoria Street,
LONDON SW1E 5JL. Tel: 0171 917 0632.

Oxfam, 274 Banbury Road, OXFORD OX2 7DZ. Tel: 01865 311311.

Population Concern, 178–202 Great Portland Street, LONDON
W1N 5TB. Tel: 0171 631 1546.

Quaker Peace and Service, Friends House, 173–7 Euston Road,
LONDON NW1 2BJ. Tel: 0171 387 3601.

Red Cross, 9 Grosvenor Crescent, LONDON SW1X 7EJ.
Tel: 0171 235 5454.

Royal Commonwealth Society for the Blind/Sight Savers,
Grosvenor Hall, Bolnore Road, HAYWARDS HEATH, West Sussex
RH16 4BX. Tel: 01444 412424

Survival International: *see* **R – RIGHTS.**

Tear Fund: *see* **C – CHILDREN.**

Tools for Self-Reliance, Netley Marsh Workshops, Netley Marsh,
SOUTHAMPTON SO40 7GY. Tel: 01703 869697.

Traidcraft Exchange, Kingsway T.V.T.E, GATESHEAD,
Tyne and Wear NE11 ONE. Tel: 0191 491 0591.

UNICEF, 55 Lincoln Inns Fields, LONDON WC2A 3NB.
Tel: 0171 405 5592.

United Nations Association (UN Association): *see*
K – KINGDOM.

Voluntary Services Overseas (VSO), 317 Putney Bridge Road,
LONDON SW15 2PN. Tel: 0181 780 2266.

Worldaware, 31 Kirby Street, LONDON EC1.
Tel: 0171 831 3844.

World Bank, 1818 H Street, NW Washington DC 20433, USA.
Tel: 202 477 1234.

World Development Movement (WDM): *see* **C – CHILDREN.**
World Vision UK: *see* **C – CHILDREN.**
Y Care International: *see* **C – CHILDREN.**

UNEMPLOYMENT

'The concept of a job for life is now obsolete.'
The research organization Mintel

Facts of the matter

- Unemployment levels in the world's industrialized nations stand at 35 million, with a further 13 million unwillingly forced into part-time work, or having given up looking for a job altogether.[1]
- Unemployment in the UK presently stands at approximately 2.5 million people, almost 10 per cent of the total workforce.
- During the 1980s boom, at least 2.5 million people were unemployed.
- Almost 1 in 10 men, and 1 in 16 women, aged 16 and over were unemployed in 1996.
- One-third of single women of working age were economically inactive in 1993 – more than twice the proportion of men.[2]
- In 1991–94, unemployment in Britain rose by 13 per cent. Long-term unemployment (i.e. a year or more) rose by 84 per cent.[3]

Introduction

Since 1979, UK unemployment figures have topped 1 million. Earlier this century, joblessness was directly linked to periods of major upheaval: the 1930s Depression, or the post-war years when returning soldiers had outgrown their pre-war work or, conversely, wanted it back – forcing out the women who had kept the furnaces burning along with the home fires.

Today, technological change, shifts in the pattern of world trade, and alterations in the way we work have promoted the rise in unemployment levels. In the West, women have taken a stronger position in the paid workforce and shaken up the employment figures in the process. Cutbacks in the manufacturing industries such as shipbuilding have left whole communities to flounder on the UK's economic scrapheap. People who are out of work spend longer without a job, and there has been an overall deterioration in employment prospects. Even a degree or a high IQ give no job guarantee.

While many people work long, stressful hours and have little time to enjoy their wealth, the unemployed have masses of enforced 'leisure time', but live in poverty. While the 1980s saw the rise of moneyed 'DINKY' ('Double Income No Kids') households, one in five households today are forced to exist on social security benefits. The Western world is moving towards the employment formula of '$\frac{1}{2}$ x 2 x 3' – that is, half as many people, working twice as hard, producing three times as much. The remainder, are left with the poorly paid, mundane jobs – or without any work at all.

For most, being unemployed cuts into the heart. On a low income, people soon feel worthless in a society that is money-led. Jobs are important for many people's self-respect, social life, and sense of contributing to the society in which they live. Made in God's image, human beings are naturally creative, and their instinct is stifled when there is no fulfilling occupation available.

Unemployment is not someone else's problem; it can happen to any one of us. Feeling let down by society, some will turn to crime as an expression of their sense of hopelessness, and to gain more money and a certain sort of respect. Others will lose faith in the system altogether and may simply opt out, or actually work to bring about its downfall. The issue of unemployment is an open wound that ultimately causes pain within the whole of our society. Able people with skills and talents that could be used to better the world, are simply left to rot.

> 'Three million unemployed is a price worth paying to reduce inflation.'

This remark by the then Chancellor of the Exchequer, Norman Lamont, reflected the difficulty of resolving conflicting goals, and the Conservative government's priority of achieving low inflation above all else. Yet it is ultimately shortsighted and callous to accept high unemployment figures in order that the majority of the population can do well, and to do so ignores the sheer pain of being jobless and the hardship it imposes on families and communities. High unemployment also destabilizes democracy, for those in power lose respect and authority from the jobless, and the drop in people's income stifles trade and the economy at local, national and global levels.

> 'The unemployed are the underclass.'

Economically, unemployed people are close to the bottom of the pile, yet the jobless represent people of all classes, qualifications and professions. It is very wrong to lump them together with newspaper reports of the 'unemployed hooligan' or the 'dole cheat'.

In the Third World, unemployment is an urban and middle-class phenomenon. With no social security system, most will beg, shoe-shine, make handicrafts or farm, or are involved in illegal activities – prostitution, drug pushing, petty theft and confidence tricks – to make ends meet.

> 'If people really want a job, they can get one.'

Whole communities joined the dole queue when mines closed down in the mid-1980s. Similarly, middle-aged people who are trained for one profession find it difficult to adapt to another when made redundant; and graduates are often classed as overqualifed for unskilled work. People who leave home in search of work, becoming 'intentionally homeless', can lose housing benefit to tide them over while they search for a job.

Many people simply cannot afford to come off the dole; and a look-round any Job Centre will reveal companies, many of them profitable enough to be household names, prepared to offer employees a scandalous rate of less than £5 an hour. Take-home pay could ultimately be less than unemployment benefit, housing benefit and council tax benefit combined. People who do part-time work until they find full-time jobs lose whatever they earn from Income Support.

Every so often, an MP decides to show the nation that the level of unemployment benefit is enough to make ends meet, and for a week they hold back on drawing from their large salary and live at the level of benefit. Invariably, at the end of the week they declare that they managed with little difficulty. Most of us probably *could* live on the dole for a week, but that doesn't take account of the *ongoing* expenses of living: toiletries, shoes, underwear, bills and so on.

ACTION COUNTDOWN

'It would be easy for the Christian realizing that industry is not controlled locally or even nationally to feel so powerless as to either try to ignore the problem of unemployment or, if his conscience does not allow this, just to join the growing voice of protest. I feel if we are able we must do more than this. Following the example of the Good Samaritan we must support or initiate action to help those hurt by the effects of unemployment. Following the example of Nehemiah we must pray and stir into action those in positions of power who can change a society that allows unemployment to play such havoc. Perhaps we can take encouragement from people like William Wilberforce who attacked the scourge of slavery with its national and international implications.' Roger Sainsbury, for the Frontier Youth Trust

- **Be sensitive.**
  Do not recklessly throw money around without a thought for the less-moneyed in your midst, nor treat the unemployed as charity cases.
- **Look out for job advertisements that may suit unemployed friends.**
  Check through the papers you read, and pass on details of your relevant contacts too.
- **Invite your unemployed friends home for a meal and company.**
  Many jobless people feel socially and economically isolated. Provide transport too.

- **Without identifying yourself, send a week's tithe to a jobless person.**
  A cheque received out of the blue will help people stay out of debt, or be used for a rare treat.
- **Financially fast.**
  Live for a month at unemployment benefit level, and give the surplus to a poverty action group.
- **Work to rule.**
  Too many companies expect their staff to work beyond their contracted hours for no extra pay. Too many employees do not question this practice, and hence many people are without work because of it.
- **If you and your partner work full time, halve your total working hours.**
  Reduce your standard of living, and give others the chance of a job.
- **Leave the country.**
  Create a job vacancy by working overseas with an agency supporting the world's poor.
- **If you're an employer, take your pick of staff from those without jobs.**
  Treat employees with respect, and pay them a take-home wage that is above full-benefit level.
- **Run a business centre from your church.**
  Invest in people and work that supports the needs of the local community.

MAKING CONTACT

See **P – POVERTY.**

Charity People Employment Agency: *see* **K – KINGDOM.**

Christians Abroad, 1 Stockwell Green, LONDON SW9 9HP.
  Tel: 0171 737 7811.

Christian Vocations: *see* **K – KINGDOM.**

VIDEO VIOLENCE

'The possibility that innocence can be corrupted, that human nature can be brutalized is a constant preoccupation of the British Board of Film Classification. We want to protect children from fear, and potential delinquents from anti-social behaviour.'

James Ferman, President of the British Board of Film Classification

Facts of the matter

- Domestic violence accounts for a quarter of all reported violent crime in the UK. Almost 50 per cent of all murders of women are killings by a current or former partner.[1]
- The approximately 3,000 research studies done on the correlation between film violence and violent behaviour conclude that there is some small effect. Less than 5 per cent of all violent behaviour is directly linked to watching films, but this remains difficult to prove.
- *The Deerhunter* is the film most linked to violent incidents in the USA, where a number of children played Russian Roulette with their parents' guns after watching the film.
- John Hinckley – who, obsessed with the actress Jodie Foster, tried to assassinate Ronald Reagan – is said to have watched the film *Taxi Driver* 15 times.[2]
- The more *realistic* the violence, the more controversy is aroused – however many deaths are shown, and however they occur.
- In 1996, 9 per cent of people watching '18' videos were aged 4–15, falling to 2 per cent aged under 10.[3]

Introduction

Concern about the impact of violent films on the promotion of violent behaviour came to a head in spring 1992 in the wake of the murder of two-year-old James Bulger at the hands of two

117

11-year-old boys, though no mention was made during the trial of any film's involvement in the crime. Coinciding with the publication of Michael Medved's book entitled *Hollywood Versus America* (1992) and the film release of Quentin Tarentino's *Reservoir Dogs* (1991), the fear of film violence seemed to reach an all-time high, and has continued to rage at intervals since then.

Concern about cinema's violent nature has been voiced since its dawn over 100 years ago. Yet violence was present before then, and in a century split in half by the Holocaust, it would surely be wrong to promote film as a scapegoat for society's ills. Christians must keep abreast of contemporary culture and attempt to understand its messages. Many films *do* contain a bleak nihilistic vision that gives no hope beyond the here and now and, in that context, a shoot-to-kill policy can be seen as a valid choice. However, Christians too must beware of a knee-jerk response to realistic violence such as that portrayed in *Reservoir Dogs*, while quietly ignoring the arguably more offensive aimed-at-children *Home Alone*. The latter, a comedy, centred on a neglected child who resorts to violently using household objects (a blow-torch, an iron, nails, Christmas baubles) in an attempt to protect himself from burglars.

People of faith must grapple with the tough issues while searching for the truth. It is incredibly difficult to prove that a particular film caused an individual to commit a violent crime. Both the Bible and J. D. Salinger's book *Catcher in the Rye* have been implicated in murder. If a link *could* be determined and violent films duly censored, this would make little impact on the violence in our society. To emphasize that violent films brutalize people is to ignore the day-to-day pressures of everyday life that grind people down.

> 'While I think there is a link between films and violence, there are more things that are linked to violence that people don't want to talk about. They tend to blame films or television rather than the things which are more potent, and if one is going to enter a rational debate about dealing with violence it would appear more rational to deal with the things that cause a higher percentage – poverty, desperation, availability of weapons etc.'
>
> Psychiatrist Dr Raj Persaud, who specializes in the effects of violent films on viewers

> 'You can't go wrong with Disney.'

There have been enough evil queens and grisly stepmothers to have left most adults with at least one terrifying childhood memory of Walt Disney's animation. The values inherent in the films should also be questioned. Disney heroines are getting stronger by the year, but the princes are almost invariably white, blond and handsome. The animal kingdom is more cutesy than red in tooth and claw, and when it does turn nasty it is because creatures have been given *human* traits. And what has become the annual Disney film 'tie-in merchandizing frenzy' is extremely successful at spreading consumerism among young children.

> 'It's safe to watch before the nine o'clock watershed.'

Before nine o'clock in the evening, there *will* be material shown that many would regard as unsuitable for children; it simply increases in amount up to the watershed. Some might find Channel 4's output more offensive than the other channels, but should be mindful of a late 1980s survey that discovered that levels of swear words were higher on average on the independent channels. However, what kept the BBC figures *low* was not that BBC1 was cleaner than the other stations (in fact it rivalled Channel 4), but that BBC2 obscenity was negligible.

> 'That awful *Child's Play* video caused those kids to murder Jamie Bulger.'

As we have already mentioned, the issue of violent videos was never raised during the actual court case. In his summing-up, though, the judge wondered aloud if videos might be to blame. The tabloid press discovered that one of the boys' fathers had rented *Child's Play III*, yet nothing proved that either 11-year-old had watched it. Sadly children do kill children. The Kray twins have admitted carrying out their first murder when they were 11. The 1952 shooting on a Croydon factory rooftop of a policeman by 16-year-old Christopher Craig, an incident that led to the hanging of the older but mentally retarded Derek Bentley, was linked to Craig's hero-worship of James Cagney. Juvenile delinquency was a major issue at that time, but few made any connection with the heavy wartime bombing of Croydon, a strategic target because of its airport, and that both boys had also been pulled out of the rubble and possibly been left psychologically scarred.

> *'When children are implicated in evil behaviour, the search for scapegoats is understandable, since it stops us facing the truth that children are not born good.'*
>
> James Ferman, President of the British Board of Film Classification

---

'It's the government's responsibility to
tighten viewing restrictions.'

Concern about the age of viewers and the suitability of material is not new, as the British Board of Film Classification certification exemplifies. Growth in television sales, and the introduction of video, though, has fuelled debate. The Video Recordings Act is only able to impose restrictions at the time of purchase. A government clamp-down would place severe restrictions on the 75 per cent of households without a child under 16.

ACTION COUNTDOWN

> *'Be wise as serpents – and gentle as doves.'*
>
> Jesus Christ

- **Go to the cinema.**
  And help children you know to appreciate this world of magic.
- **Make television viewing a family affair.**
  Take television sets out of children's bedrooms so that everyone watches together.
- **Why don't you turn off your television set and go and do something else instead?**
  Use the 'off' button more often: read a book; phone or meet a friend. Be *creative*.
- **Go for a week without watching television – or using computer games.**
  Simply switch off – and wonder what you missed.

- **Learn to discern.**
  Be selective. Read reviews and identify the critics whose views you respect.
- **Live without a television.**
  Good newspaper critics will keep you informed. Find time and space for an active life.
- **Be an intelligent viewer.**
  Avoid kneejerk reactions. Instead, consider a film's message and context.
- **Use videos as a conversation starter.**
  Discuss with friends and family what you are watching and the issues raised.
- **Make friends with your local video dealer.**
  Compliment them on their positive choices, and encourage them away from stocking 'nasties'.
- **Show films in your church hall, and invite the public.**
  Hire films that speak of redemption and *joie de vivre*, regardless of whether they were made by Christians.

MAKING CONTACT

BBC Television, Wood Lane, LONDON W12. Tel (*Duty Officer*): 0181 743 8000.

British Board of Film Classification (BBFC), 3 Soho Square, LONDON W1V 6HD. Tel: 0171 439 7961.

British Film Institute (BFI), 21 Stephen Street, LONDON W1P 2LN. Tel: 0171 255 1444.

Broadcasting Standards Council (BSC): *see* **L – LETTERS.**

Channel 4, 124 Horseferry Road, LONDON SW1P 2TX. Tel: 0171 306 8333.

European Leisure Software Publishers Association (ELSPA), Suite 1, Haddonsacre, Station Road, Offenham, EVESHAM, Worcester WR11 5LW. Tel: 01386 830642.

Fraser Steel, Head of the Programmes Complaints Unit BBC: *see* **L – LETTERS.**

Independent Television Commission: *see* **L – LETTERS.**

London Weekend Television, South Bank Television Centre, Kent House, Upper Ground, LONDON SE1. Tel (*Viewers' Correspondence*): 0171 620 1620.

National Viewers and Listeners' Association, All Saints House, High Street, COLCHESTER, Essex CO1 1UG. Tel: 01206 561155.

Radio Authority: *see* **L – LETTERS.**

Video Standards Council (VSC), Kinetic Business Centre, Theobold Street, BOREHAMWOOD, Herts WD6 4SE. Tel: 0181 387 4020

Viewer and Listener Correspondence, BBC: *see* **L – LETTERS**.

Voice of the Listener and Viewer (Mrs Jocelyn Hay), 101 Kings Drive, GRAVESEND, Kent DA12 5BQ.

WAR

'If our country's cause is the cause of God, wars must be wars of annihilation. A false transcendence is given to things which are very much of this world.'

C. S. Lewis

Facts of the matter

- Since 1945, there have been over 120 armed conflicts throughout the world.
- The world's main arms exporters, accounting for 86 per cent of sales to the Third World, are the five permanent members of the UN Security Council: USA, Russia, UK, France, China.
- Of the 82 armed conflicts in 1991–94, 79 were within individual countries.
- Over 105 million unexploded landmines remain in 62 countries as a legacy of war.
- Some 35,000 men, women and children, mostly civilians, have lost one or more limbs, largely as a result of the 6–10 million landmines that remained after Cambodia's 25-year-long civil war; 1 in 236 people is an amputee.
- Around 24 million people have been displaced in their own countries because of civil war.[1]
- From 1980–90, almost three-quarters of the arms used by Somali dictator Siad Barre came from the USA. During this time, Somalia was spending 5 times as much on the military as on health and education put together – the highest ratio in the world.[2]
- Third World debt is now the single largest contributory factor to global instability, and at least one-fifth of such debt is incurred by buying weapons.
- The 'peace dividend' from the 1987–94 cuts in military spending produced $935 billion – $810 billion of this in industrial nations – yet it effectively vanished, used to pay off budget deficits rather than being used for developmental or environmental programmes.

Introduction

We live in a violent, warmongering world. The history of humanity is one of battle between communities of difference; it is one of the most obvious signs of humanity's base nature. Yet ironically, the Church of the Prince of Peace has not always been quick to stand outside the conflict. Throughout its history, the Christian Church has at times little differed from the way of the world. During the Second World War, plenty of Christians in Germany and Austria regarded the Third Reich as God-ordained – or at least a perfectly justifiable New Order. (In their view, the Jews were simply getting their come-uppance for crucifying Christ.) During the Falklands and Gulf wars, any UK Church voice against the action was quiet, and most believers became caught up in the nationalism that swept the country. As ex-CND head Bruce Kent has pointed out, those who question the option of war at such times are regarded as unpatriotic.

When *any* lives are at stake, Christians must stand back from the general consensus and stop to think and pray about the view they should take. The issue of whether a particular call to arms is a 'just war' (or if there *is* such a thing as a just war) must be a major initial consideration. Possible options for Christians will range from pacifism, through civil disobedience and non-violent direct action, to fighting for a cause or one's country as a fully paid-up member of the armed forces. Whatever position one takes, Christians must remain aware of the evil that is intrinsic to the act of war. The first casualty of war, it has been said, is truth. In being true to God, Christians must seek to act against the lies that spread, and aim to foster forgiveness, love and understanding throughout the human race.

> 'Thou shalt not kill.'

For many Christians, Jesus' teaching is clear-cut. For them, war is always wrong and there are no circumstances in which violence can be justified. Pacifists thus also avoid being the pawns in other people's wargames, conscientiously objecting to conscription. Christians who accept the doctrine of the just war in the fight against sheer evil must take care in using it to justify their country's involvement in any of the world's war zones.

Any war comes as a result of failed diplomacy or people missing vital signs of aggression that preceded the conflict. The arms trade has complicated matters in its bid to sell products in a post-Cold War flooded market; before the Gulf War, the UK sold weapons to Iraq. There are occasions when intervention is admirable and justifiable, when to do otherwise would provoke a greater evil. Yet we must note too the long-occupied nations such as Tibet or East Timor where our government is less vocal about injustice, and wonder why these peoples do not receive outside support.

'War is always a descent into barbarism. It is evil. To dignify it as "just" when its causes, methods and results are always and inevitably unjust is to abuse language. War can only be justified because the best possible estimate of all the available alternatives indicates that not to go to war would be even more unjust.'

Philip Crowe, in *A Whisper Will Be Heard* (Fount, 1994)

> 'Jesus didn't tell the soldiers he met to leave the army.'

Jesus' dealings with the military in occupied Palestine tell us something about faith and integrity; a soldier is prepared to follow Jesus' teachings without quibbling for he understands what it means to live by another's command. Yet at no time does Jesus tell these men of war, 'This isn't the life for you. Go away and live peacefully.'

God speaks to individuals where they are – and some he will lead elsewhere, and others will be of value in their original chosen field. If there has to be a defence force or a war it is perhaps better that there are people of God in the frontline living and working in the world's tough spots. Other Christians' lifestyles might contradict our choices, but with prayer and discernment we must live and let live, taking care not to judge others and their motives.

> 'Don't we need defending?'

It is pertinent to ask what is being defended. A third of the UK's children live in poverty, approximately 2.5 million people are unemployed, the nation's manufacturing industries have closed down, and its state operations are sold to the highest bidder. The British government spends twice as much of its taxpayers' money on the military than its major European allies, while its welfare and foreign aid budgets are consistently reduced. If our country needs defending, it is not from some dark external force, but from government policies that take no account of how people really live, and our apathy that makes little protest.

> 'Surely a nuclear deterrent is vital.'

Even those who suffered under the Japanese during the Second World War in August 1945 believe that the dropping of the bombs on Hiroshima and Nagasaki was a wicked action. It has long been argued that the Japanese were about to surrender, and Churchill stated that Japan's defeat was certain before the first bomb fell, 'brought about by overwhelming maritime power . . .' In the UK, the very build-up of the Trident nuclear arsenal contravened the Non-Proliferation Treaty – revealing the difficulty of controlling weapons.

> 'Isn't there a need to help foreign governments
> deal with civil unrest?'

Not all governments are democratically elected or have the best interests of their people at heart. The British government's export of weapons to oppressive regimes such as China, Indonesia or Nigeria, supports systems that eliminate those who oppose them. The European Council *does* include the 'respect of human rights in the country of final destination' as one of its arms export criteria, but members do not stick to the rules. In June 1995, the British Foreign Office revealed that it had issued licences to export CS gas and rubber bullets to the Nigerian police, a force that abuses human rights, and that used the weaponry on pro-democracy demonstrations. Money spent by Third World countries on Western arms is also money taken away from health, education and the local economy.

'Let Britain end its support for dictatorships.'
Wole Soyinka, Nigerian Nobel prizewinner

> 'What about unemployment if we get rid of the arms trade?'

Rather than keeping highly skilled personnel locked within an industry (which denies that its product is designed to kill people), the arms trade ultimately *creates* unemployment.

Defence products are expensive to make and often sell for less than their cost of production. The arms industry is therefore heavily subsidized by the public's taxes via defence ministry contracts that could have been better spent on more labour-intensive and wealth-creative enterprises. In the USA, taxpayers pay for up to one-third of all US weapons sold because their government, like others in the West, underwrites loans and gives 'export credits' to ensure sales to potential buyers of weapons. In 1989, the UK government gave export credits to cover $9.75 million of machine tools bound for an Iraqi chemical weapons factory, and it is unlikely that Iraqi leader Saddam Hussein will ever pay for it.

ACTION COUNTDOWN

'Blessed are the Peacemakers for they shall be called the children of God.'

Jesus Christ

- **Listen, think, pray, and aim to love and understand.**
  The fight against war begins in our hearts, and in our everyday dealings with other people.
- **Pay your respects by visiting your local war memorials.**
  Consider what the loss of these people must have meant, and still means, to the community.
- **Buy a poppy – and wear it in remembrance.**
  The Poppy Factory's 34 million poppies and 100,000 wreaths help needy ex-servicemen.
- **Join the World Council of Churches' Programme to Overcome Violence (see Making Contact section).**
  Support its campaign to promote peace issues to individuals, churches and communities.
- **Using the Bibliography on page 166, read books and poems by those involved in war.**
  Aim to understand and empathize with people trapped by conflict.

127

- **Read the international news section of the quality press.**
  Keep abreast of world-wide conflicts and pray for the people involved.
- **Write to your MP.**
  One government department, the Defence Export Services Organization, exists solely to promote arms sales. Demand that Britain stop selling arms to repressive regimes, whether directly or indirectly, *now*. Request that money be spent on aid, not arms.
- **Write to your bank.**
  Demand assurances that they do not finance arms sales.
- **Visit your local British Legion headquarters.**
  Talk to those who fought for their country; listen to their experiences.
- **Convert swords into ploughshares.**
  If you work for the arms industry or the Forces, use your training in another field. Highly skilled technicians are vital to modern medicine; small-scale industry vital to redundant communities thrives with the focus and discipline that you could bring.

MAKING CONTACT

Campaign Against the Arms Trade (CAAT), 11 Goodwin Street, LONDON N4 3HQ. Tel: 0171 281 0297.

Campaign for Nuclear Disarmament (CND), 162 Holloway Road, LONDON N7 8DQ. Tel: 0171 700 2393.

Imperial War Museum, Lambeth Road, LONDON SE1 6HZ. Tel: 0171 416 5000.

Ploughshares Action. (For details of non-violent direct action campaigns, contact **Campaign Against the Arms Trade**.)

Programme to Overcome Violence, Peace Desk – International Affairs, Programme Unit III, Justice, Peace & Creation, World Council of Churches, PO Box 2100, CH-1211 Geneva 2, Switzerland.

Royal British Legion, 48 Pall Mall, LONDON SW1Y 5JY. Tel: 0171 973 7200.

United Nations Association (UN Association): *see* **K – KINGDOM.**

World Development Movement (WDM): *see* **C – CHILDREN.**

XENOPHOBIA

'Everyone has the right to seek and to enjoy in other countries asylum from persecution.'

UN Universal Declaration of Human Rights

Facts of the matter

- There are over 20 million refugees world-wide, half of whom are children. Some 80 per cent of refugees are women and children.
- In 1994, an estimated 750,000 refugees and asylum seekers fled the ethnic conflict of former Yugoslavia. Approximately 2 million refugees fled Rwanda, away from its bloody civil war.
- Each year, up to 30 million people are forced to move because of environmental problems and poverty.
- In 1950, the population of Mexico City was 3.5 million. By the year 2000, it is expected to be 25.6 million.
- Between 1983 and 1992, an estimated 139,000 people applied for asylum in the UK.
- Some 7.3 per cent of young ethnic people in the UK become homeless as a result of their parents returning to their homeland.
- In the UK, the number of black children excluded from school is disproportionate to the number of whites. In parts of the UK, black children are 6 times more likely to be expelled.[1]
- According to Metropolitan Police Commissioner Paul Condon, 80 per cent of London's mugging could be attributed to black men.
- London's Camden Borough has the worst record for racial violence in Britain. In the first half of 1995, there were 271 reported incidents of racial attacks, with the majority of victims being Bengali.[2]

Introduction

The world's people are a 'floating population'; few people in England, for example, will have an entirely English pedigree. In this century alone, two world wars brought a mass of nationalities to our island, a request to the Commonwealth for extra workforce brought more in the 1950s, and the shift of races world-wide continues unabated for a variety of other reasons.

Across the world, it is often the consequences of living in poverty, a deteriorating environment or the threat of war that forces people beyond their local community, and also their country's boundaries, in search of a better life. Yet it is to neighbour states to which most people flee, or to countries that have an historical connection – thus Algerians will be invited to France to work, Turks to Germany, Jamaicans to Britain, for example.

Yet the fear of 'foreigners' is very common wherever you live. Scratch the surface and there are few people, even the most 'politically correct', who do not bear some grudge against people not of their kind, whether in terms of race, class, sex, sexuality or religion. Discrimination will range from the blatant (for example, the landlord who asks the colour of your skin when you phone to rent a room), to the more subtle or simply patronizing, whereby people are treated as if they belong to an altogether different *species*.

This is certainly not a Christian attitude. We may have differences of opinion with one individual, we may not like the way he or she leads his or her life, but we cannot tar their entire race, sex, sexuality, class or colour with the same brush. Our role is to break down barriers rather than confirm them. Too often our churches only *mirror* society, simply reflecting class and colour divides of the world outside. We must fight peer pressure and the darkness within our own hearts to reach out and touch our neighbour, whatever their circumstance, whoever they are, for in doing so we will reveal something of God's infinite love for us and our fellow human beings.

> 'Middle-class values about racism are better than working-class ones.'

Working-class people often express themselves far more openly than Britain's traditionally reticent middle class. So when an individual makes an offensive racist comment they can be castigated by others who are in fact no less racist, but who simply communicate their feelings differently. It is the *action* that reveals the heart more often than what is said.

> 'We will not be an appendage to your plans and strategies. We must seek true partnership. Our choirs sing at your conferences and you applaud loudly. But when injustice affects our community, there is often a resounding silence from the white church.'
>
> The Reverend Ronald Nathan, General Secretary of the
> African Caribbean Evangelical Alliance

Neither is it enough to mark someone out as racist because of what they say, without making some attempt to understand what has provoked such feelings. Many white people in inner-city areas will have seen their communities change colour over a number of decades. Whether or not you agree with their viewpoint, their fears and insecurities still need to be addressed rather than ignored. If we don't address the fears of such white people, we will find that the only people who bother to make a connection with them are the political extremists looking for votes.

> 'There are too many people flooding into
> the country.'

There is a massive discrepancy between the figures of actual immigrants to the UK compared with the numbers most people *imagine* enter the country, yet this misconception fuels draconian government measures to limit immigration. Peter Lilley's 1995 Immigration and Asylum Bill is just such an example, regarding applications for asylum as generally bogus and, as in the dangerous 1930s, treating refugees within the same framework as ordinary immigrants. Often fearing for their life in their homeland, such refugees have fled to the UK, only to be ineligible for work and without social security support while seeking asylum. Christians must know the *facts* in order to help set others free from such injustices.

> 'Most muggings are committed by young black men.'

Metropolitan Police Commissioner Sir Paul Condon's declaration in July 1995 met with allegations of racism among groups trying to promote equal opportunities, and fears that the scheme to reduce street crime via Operation Eagle Eye would target black men for 'stop and search'. It was noted too that when the police were tackling football hooliganism, no mention was ever made of the perpetrators being predominantly *white* young men.

> 'Racists like the British National Party deserve any treatment they get.'

It is the aim of groups like Anti-Fascist Action and the Anti-Nazi League to ensure that the openly racist views of groups like the British National Party or National Front are not given space. While the anti-racists' motives are admirable, many of their members are prepared to employ violent means to achieve their goal. Anti-Nazi League members fighting the British National Party at Hanworth by-election in September 1995 in Hounslow's Civic Centre became national news, but it is arguable what viewers made of it.

There is an argument for freedom of speech without people being assaulted for what they say. Violence or aggression from any quarter rarely alters people's views on anything; they simply become quieter about their true beliefs. This is one of the dangers of 'political correctness', which can hide the unchanged harsh side of people's natures under a thin veneer of respectable, acceptable words. By letting people have their say, by arguing rationally with them, by enabling people with extreme views to mix with those of differing opinions, change can occur, fears can be dispelled, barriers can be broken, and space allowed for reconciliation, forgiveness, repentance, peace and love to flourish.

ACTION COUNTDOWN

*'There is neither Jew or Gentile, slave or free, man or woman. We
are all the same in Christ Jesus.'*

St Paul

- **Consider the street and town where you live and work.**
  What is its history? What nationalities and cultures are repre-
  sented?
- **Become multi-cultural.**
  Retain pride in your own culture and faith, but be open to learn-
  ing how others live.
- **Speak out against racism.**
  Silence equals agreement. Instead, break gently through barriers
  of ignorance and prejudice.
- **Open up your home.**
  Let your home be a place where people of all nationalities and
  cultures feel welcome.
- **Learn a foreign language.**
  People will appreciate that you cared enough to try to commu-
  nicate better.
- **Teach English as a foreign language.**
  Whether here or abroad, help give people a voice at a level
  where knowing English counts.
- **Welcome foreign students.**
  Invite them to stay, especially at Christmas and holiday-time. Or
  rent out a room.
- **Give practical help to asylum seekers and refugees in your
  community.**
  Help them to obtain the support they need. Be a friend in a
  strange land.
- **Set up a community centre for the local immigrant
  women.**
  Many immigrant women stay at home and know little English. A
  communal place where they can make friends, gain skills and
  improve their language gives them confidence.
- **Be a surrogate parent.**
  Many single parents of mixed-raced children need help in
  introducing their children to the culture of the children's father/
  mother. If that culture is your own, help a child to grow up
  being proud of his or her roots.

MAKING CONTACT

African Caribbean Evangelical Alliance, Whitefield House,
186 Kennington Park Road, LONDON SE11 4BT.
Tel: 0171 582 0228.

British Red Cross Society, International Welfare Department,
9 Grosvenor Crescent, LONDON SW1X 7EJ. Tel: 0171 235 5454.

Campaign Against the Immigration and Asylum Bill (CAIAB),
28 Commercial Street, LONDON E1 6LF. Tel: 0171 247 9907.

Catholic Association for Racial Justice, The Co-op Centre,
11 Mowll Street, LONDON SW9 6BG. Tel: 0171 582 2554.

Christians Aware, 10 Springfield Road, LEICESTER LE2 3BD.
Tel: 01162 708831.

Churches Commission for Racial Justice, Inter-Church House,
35 Lower Marsh, LONDON SE1 7RL. Tel: 0171 620 4444.

Commission for Racial Equality, Elliot House,
10–12 Allington Street, LONDON SW1E 5EH. Tel: 0171 828 7022.

Federation of Black Housing Organizations, 374 Grays Inn Road,
LONDON WC1X 8BB. Tel: 0171 837 8288.

Irish Support and Advice Service, Hammersmith and Fulham
Irish Centre, Black's Road, LONDON W6 9DT. Tel: 0181 741 0466.

Joint Council for the Welfare of Immigrants, 115 Old Street,
LONDON EC1V 9JR. Tel: 0171 251 8706.

Medical Foundation for the Victims of Torture,
96 Grafton Road, LONDON NW5. Tel: 0171 813 7777.

Ockenden Venture, Constitution Hill, WOKING, Surrey GU22 7UU.
Tel: 01483 772012.

Refugee Advisers Support Group: *see* **Refugee Council.**
(*Advice Line*: Tel: 0171 582 9927.)

Refugee Arrivals Project, 2005 Queen's Building,
Heathrow Airport, HOUNSLOW, Middlesex TW6 1DL.
Tel: 0181 759 5740.

Refugee Council, 3 Bondway, LONDON SW8 1SJ.
Tel: 0171 582 6922.

Refugee Legal Centre, Sussex House, 39–45 Bermondsey Street,
LONDON SE1 3XF. Tel: 0171 827 9090.

United Nations High Commissioner for Refugees (UNCHR),
PO Box 2500, 1211 GENEVA 2 Depot, Switzerland.
Tel: 022 739 8502.

YOUTH

'We may care enormously about our children but is that the same as respecting their feelings? We may worship the concept of youth but we jump to categorise youth's predicament through inane classifications. Thus they are slackers, ravers, hooligans, the blank generation. We give them their head, let them do their own thing and then feign shock that they feel adrift from adult culture. We do not understand their language nor want to and insist that conflict between one generation and the next is inevitable, even desirable. In order to grow up one has to reject your elders, we tell each other, not seeing that so many of the problems arise because they do not want to reject us but simply have us accept them.' Suzanne Moore, in the *Guardian*

Facts of the matter

- One-fifth of British men aged between 16 and 19 are unemployed.
- In 1991, 1 in 5 British 20-year-olds were innumerate, and 1 in 7 were illiterate.
- Some 68 per cent of secondary schoolchildren do less than 1.5 hours of homework a night.
- In 1993–4, there were 11,200 permanent school exclusions, three times more than in 1991–2.[1]
- A third of secondary schoolchildren watch 4 or more hours of television every day.
- An estimated 51 per cent of teenagers under the age of 16 have tried illicit drugs. Some 25 million Ecstasy tablets are taken every year in the UK; up to 50 youths die every year as a result.[2]
- In an Evangelical Coalition on Drugs survey, 10 per cent of under 16s among 7,666 church-affiliated youths aged 12–30 had tried drugs, rising to 23 per cent in the 17–30 age group.

- Of adult smokers, 5 out of 6 began smoking when they were under 16 years old.
- A quarter of prostitutes arrested in West Yorkshire's vice spots in September 1992 were aged 16 or under, a rise of 21 per cent on the previous year.[3]
- About 156,000 youths in England and Wales are homeless, a third in London with under 18,000 hostel places, claims Shelter. In 1995, 25 per cent more youths used Centrepoint's shelters.
- Approximately 1 in 3 young homeless people have been in care.

Introduction

It is too simplistic to lump together young people from teens through to the twenties into some amorphous social grouping and dismiss them with a throwaway tag. Even taking into account the shared years of schooling, there are vast differences of experiences and levels of ability even within the same *classroom*.

However, the apparent black and white certainties of their parents' generation are no more. It is not a matter of leaving school and getting a job that will last a lifetime (if that were ever actually the case). Even those who can afford to go on to university (there are no grants any more) are not guaranteed a professional post when they graduate. Already weighed down by the debt of a student loan, obtaining a mortgage and home of your own in a world where short-term employment contracts are increasingly the norm can be merely a dream. Already four times as many 16–34-year-olds than any other age group have negative equity. They also have the added burden of worrying about paying for health insurance and pension schemes that even many high-paid professionals have trouble affording. Many of these young people have seen their parents' marriage crumble – so how can they be sure about committing themselves to one person for life, for the next 60 years?

Is it any wonder that many young people seem confused or apathetic? In a world of shifting sands it is difficult to know who or what to believe any more. Some dismiss it all in a nihilistic, post-modernist 'there are no answers, rights or wrongs, what's right by you is fine by me' whirligig of half-truths. The challenge to the Church is to present Christianity in a form that gives hope amid the maelstrom, in a form that provides wisdom and truth, and a real reason for being, in a mind-blowing world of information overload.

> 'Why not reduce the school leaving age to 14?'

It is tempting to think that disruptive, ill-educated teenagers, or those who are simply bright but non-academic and bored, keen to leave school behind and earn some money might be better off in some sort of work or training and acquiring useful, practical skills. However, lowering the school leaving age can be based on a presumption of failure and a philosophy of defeat that decides that certain children are not worth educational investment.

It can be argued, in fact, that these are the very children who need more resources and assistance so that they can reach their full potential. Not only is it in their individual interests, but it is in the interests of the whole nation. Young people trained to their utmost ability ensure that the UK can stand economically alongside its European neighbours rather than be seen as a poor relation on a par with Third World manufacturers.[4]

> 'My children go to clubs, and they don't drink
> any alcohol.'

Some parents are so out of touch with contemporary youth culture that they are impressed that their offspring rely on *water* throughout all-night raves – a raging thirst being a side effect of the use of Ecstasy. While every music trend since the 1960s has had its poison, the use of Ecstasy and its availability as an integral part of the 1990s dance culture is probably unprecedented. Its casual use belies the fact the long-term effects on the user's mind, body and spirit are not yet known. The cities of Hamburg and Berlin report liver damage and the need for liver transplants among users, and because, like depressives, those who take Ecstasy have lower levels of the hormone seratonin in their spinal fluid, there is a possibility of higher rates of suicide and depression. Overheating and dehydration increase the risk of death. Additionally, users will experiment with other drugs: amphetamines for highs, Ecstasy to get energy, and cannabis to come down slowly. Adults need to keep abreast of modern trends and be open with teenagers about the risks involved.

> 'They just hang around street corners,
> up to no good.'

Teenagers are poised on the brink of finding a secure footing in the adult world, but it is often a scary place from their perspective – and their actions will fluctuate unsteadily from novice attempts to be mature to a reversion to the security of childhood. It is a place where we have all been, and we need to remember this when we are ready to denounce adolescents.

Today's teenagers are not helped by severe limitations on where they can go and what they can do. Outside the confines of sports clubs and established groups such as the Scouts or Guides, there is little for them to do with their friends in the evenings outside home. Pubs and clubs will understandably restrict their entry, and many teenagers resort to buying canned drinks from off-licences and drinking it on the streets. Adults must make a concerted effort to provide safe venues where young people are respected and can relax and be themselves.

> 'Today's youth are less caring than previous
> generations.'

To write off an entire section of our population as belonging to Generation X is to ignore the contribution that so many young people make to the community in which they live. While statistics reveal that the under-25s are four times less likely to be registered to vote than any other eligible group, this is as much a sign of disillusionment with a parliamentary system that they feel ignores their needs as it is a sign of political apathy. The people who did so much to raise money for Africa by buying Band Aid singles, and spending what was then a whopping £25 to attend the Live Aid concert, are the very people at the top end of the so-called Blank Generation. Additionally, plenty of teenagers are very politically active, but their views are demeaned within the main party political forum. Animal rights and the environment are key issues of interest to young people, and both have been traditionally devalued by both Church and parliamentarians as of minority concern. Yet such political concern reveals a high level of youthful idealism, enthusiasm and faith in the ability to change the world for the better.

ACTION COUNTDOWN

> *'We must look not just for the conversion of individuals but for the transformation of groups of teenagers in the light of the Gospel. From these friendship groups a distinctive Christian culture can emerge.'*
>
> Pete Ward, in *Youth Culture and the Gospel*
> (Marshall Pickering, 1992)

- **Become aware of teenagers.**
  Make a point of looking out for those in your midst as a starting point in understanding them.
- **Consider their place in the scheme of things.**
  Is your community youth friendly? How are they viewed by others? Is this fair? Discuss.
- **Make a list of local young people's haunts.**
  What do they do all day? Are there any obvious gaps in provision for them?
- **Find out about their lifestyle and taste in music, fashion and sport.**
  Reveal your interest not to show young people how in touch you are (teenagers are never impressed by adults trying to be cool), but in order to love, and to learn from them.
- **Be prepared to listen.**
  Give young people space to be themselves. Take seriously their feelings and experiences.
- **Zoom in on young people's political perspective.**
  Develop a Christian response to teenage concerns for the environment and animal rights.
- **Invite young people into your home.**
  Whether you have a family or not, cross the generation gap by welcoming them in.
- **Start up a church youth group and drop-in centre.**
  Use your knowledge of local youth lifestyle and needs to develop a relevant place to be.

- **Set up an Alternative Worship Service.**
  To attract teenagers to church, develop a programme that reflects their culture.
- **Train as a youth leader or teacher.**
  Use your skills to help put young people on the right path for life.

MAKING CONTACT

Adfam National Helpline re drug use: Tel: 0171 928 8900.

Centrepoint: *see* **H – HOMELESSNESS.**

Exploring Parenthood, 20a Treadgold Street, LONDON W11. Tel: 0171 221 4471.

Freephone Drug Problems. Dial 100.

Frontier Centre, 70–74 City Road, LONDON EC1Y 2BJ. Tel: 0171 336 7744.

Frontier Youth Trust: *see* **C – CHILDREN.**

ISDD (Institute for the Study of Drug Dependence): *see* **SCODA** for address. Tel: 0171 928 1211.

Release Drugs Advice Line. Tel: 0171 729 9904.

Release 24 hour Emergency Line. Tel: 0171 603 8654.

Re-Solv (The Society for the Prevention of Solvent and Volatile Substance Abuse), 30a High Street, STONE, Staffordshire ST15 8AW. Tel: 01785 817885.

SCODA (Standing Conference on Drug Abuse), Waterbridge House, 32–36 Loman Street, LONDON SE1 OEE. Tel: 0171 928 9500.

Scottish Drugs Forum, 5 Waterloo Street, GLASGOW G2 6AY. Tel: 0141 221 1175.

Scripture Union: *see* **C – CHILDREN.**

TACADE (The Advisory Council on Alcohol and Drug Education), 1 Hulme Place, The Crescent, SALFORD, Greater Manchester M5 4QA. Tel: 0161 745 8925.

UK Forum on Young People and Gambling, PO Box 5, CHICHESTER, West Sussex PO19 3RB. Tel: 01243 538635.

Welsh Office Drugs Unit, Welsh Office, Crown Building, Cathays Park, CARDIFF CF1 3NQ. Tel: 01222 825111.

Who Cares? Trust, 152–160 City Road, LONDON EC1V 2NP. Tel: 0171 251 3117.

YMCA, 640 Forest Road, LONDON E17 3DZ. Tel: 0181 520 5599.

ZOOLOGY

'To say that we love God and at the same time exercise cruelty towards the least creature is a contradiction in itself.'

John Woolman, 1720–72

Facts of the matter

- Fewer than 200 Siberian tigers are left, and fewer than 80 South China tigers. Sumatran tigers total 650 at most. Indo-Chinese tigers number 800–1,750, with 4,700 Bengal tigers based mostly in India. 'And that's it. That's all the tigers that are left in the wild. The Bali tiger disappeared in the 1940s. There has been no sign of the Caspian tiger since the early 1970s. And no confirmation of the Javan tiger since about 1980.'[1]
- In 20 years, the number of black rhino has plummeted from 60,000 to just 2,500.
- Only 600 mountain gorillas remain.
- The Brown Bear, extinct in Britain since the tenth century, is virtually extinct throughout Western Europe. Only 8–10 are left in France.[2]
- Some 30 million square miles of ocean around Antarctica have been declared a whale sanctuary.
- Annually, Britain exports almost 2 million live sheep and lambs and 500,000 young calves to Europe. The veal calves will be reared under conditions banned in the UK.[3]
- Around 30 million battery hens in Britain are kept in cages too small to enable the birds to spread their wings. Nearly half a million pigs are kept in concrete stalls, unable to turn around. Millions more turkeys, chickens and rabbits are also kept in factory farms throughout their lives. About 700 million animals are killed for food every year in slaughterhouses.[4]
- Of the 20 million or so lambs born each year, some 4 million die in the first few days of life from exposure, disease or malnutrition.[5]

141

- Human morbidity – and per capita consumption of pharmaceuticals – continues to rise despite 90 years of intensive research on animals. Drugs are suspected of causing 19,000 adverse effects annually in the UK – probably only a tenth of the true figure.[6]

Introduction

It is crisis time for some of the rarest of mammals. Precious habitats are burned, polluted or destroyed to serve humanity's perceived needs, and there is nowhere left for wild animals to hide. Christians should be concerned that God's creation, which he pronounced 'good', is being plundered. They are his creatures whose numbers are being decimated in our name.

Many animal lives are wasted, or passed in ways that reduce existence to mere economic units – and completely contrary to that for which God created them. Genetic engineering and growth hormones are used to produce more meat, or even organs for human transplantation. Luxury products, such as cosmetics and ever more abundant household cleaners, are tested on animals. Where there may be some reason for vivisection for medical research, there remains tremendous duplication of tests, not primarily for the benefit of science and humankind, but in order that drug companies can be first with the results.

Jesus made it quite clear that his Father cares for wildlife and its habitats, for the birds of the air and the lilies of the fields, as much as for the human race. There is a hierarchy of creation – the health of one man's mind was worth more than a herd of swine – but *our* duty is not to use this knowledge to benefit ourselves, but to value the world around us. It was after the Fall that chaos closed in and animals began to fear humanity. To work towards God's Kingdom is to work to close divisions so that one day the lion will lie down with the lamb.

'Christians are called to act respectfully towards "these, the least of our brothers and sisters". This is not a simple question of kindness ... it is an issue of strict justice. The ethic for the liberation of life requires that we render unto animals what they are due, as creatures with an independent integrity and

value. Precisely because they cannot speak for themselves, the Christian duty to speak and act for them is the greater, not the lesser.'

The Church and Society Consultation of
the World Council of Churches

'Why worry about animals when human beings suffer so much world-wide?'

'It's not that I'm more interested in animals than humans, I'm just interested in life,' explained Bill Travers, the late one-time actor who was to co-found Zoo Check (now the Born Free Foundation). Often an individual's concern for animals is interpreted as an alternative to showing compassion for human beings, while this need not be so.

What is done to animals has a knock-on effect on humans. Medicines, medical techniques and cosmetics tested on animals will eventually be tested on human beings. A poison or virus entering the food chain, such as BSE or DDT, could affect people who eat animal flesh. Third World malnutrition would be reduced if the West did not plunder vital foodstuffs like grain and fish stocks to feed their livestock. And, anyway, animals as part of God's creation must be treated with respect.

'Vegetarianism isn't biblical.'

Before the Fall, the human race ate no meat. After the Flood, Noah was told that it was now acceptable, but that animals would live in fear. There is nothing wrong *per se* with eating meat, but being a meat-eater is certainly not a symbol of righteousness, as some Christians have claimed. World-wide, regular meat-eating is a luxury few can afford, or have ever been able to afford. In the British Isles it was not until the nineteenth century that meat became the regular diet of most people.

Many deeply committed Christians become vegetarians simply because they *are* deeply committed Christians. They care about the cruel way God's creatures are treated; they are deeply aware of the knock-on effect of the commercial exploitation of animals. In fact, with such information, unless one eats meat reared organically, there is in this country very good reason for Christians to choose vegetarianism over remaining omnivorous.

'Animals are only here for our use.'

When human beings are regarded as the pinnacle of evolutionary development or morally and spiritually apart from the rest of creation, it is not difficult to regard humanity as sole beneficiaries of all we survey. In economic terms, the words 'progress' and 'development' take their cue from such a philosophy; the world is ours to plunder as we choose.

Yet this misunderstanding is dangerous on two counts. If animals are ultimately regarded as little more than economic units, then short cuts in their care will be taken. Already animals are genetically engineered and farmed intensively to ensure high productivity. The stress, hormonal additives and high productivity diets are passed on through the food chain to the human consumer. And to regard animals as here solely for our use is to ignore God's love of his creation. It was deemed 'good' long before we came on the scene, and Jesus reiterates this, explaining how God feeds the birds of the trees; they are in his care.

'Suppose you had to have a kidney transplant?'

Anybody who opposes animal vivisection will at some point be questioned as to what they would do if faced with a serious health condition, the subtext being that it was through just such animal experimentation that successful treatment for humans was developed.

While there is truth in this, there is also strong evidence of damage to humans caused through vivisection. Neither animal tests of thalidomide, or the anti-arthritis drug Opren, revealed how dangerous they were for human use. Not only do different species respond differently to medical treatment and drugs, but so do individual *people*. All drugs, which by their very nature are to some degree poisonous, will at some point be tested on humans – regardless of how many animals have been used in research. Only then can any reliable indication of its capabilities be obtained – yet that will not take account of long-term effects.

144

'Let the law of kindness know no limits. Show a loving considera-tion for all God's creatures.'

General Advices and Queries of the Society of Friends, 1931

- **Find out more.**
  Write for leaflets and further information from the organizations listed in the Making Contact section.
- **Visit your local pet shop, circus or zoo.**
  Pray for the animals in captivity, that they may roam free in heaven.
- **Boycott companies that test cosmetics on animals.**
  Plenty of harmless alternatives are available. Write to PETA (see the Making Contact section) for further information.
- **Choose a cruelty-free diet.**
  Eat free-range eggs and meat that has been reared in natural surroundings and organically produced rather than intensively farmed. Choose not to eat at restaurants that serve veal.
- **Become a vegetarian.**
  Leave meat off the menu. Consider non-leather alternatives to what you wear too.
- **Adopt a domestic pet that needs a home.**
  Visit your local animal sanctuary and take home a pet that might otherwise be put down.
- **Adopt a wild animal via the Born Free Foundation (see the Making Contact section).**
  Write for details of their various adoption schemes for animals such as chimpanzees, elephants, wolves and schools of whales that live in sanctuaries and on reserves.
- **Organize a service of animal thanksgiving, intercession and blessing.**
  Have people bring their pets and livestock to church.
- **Support humane research.**
  If you are a medical researcher, opt for work that makes no use of animals; the Dr Hadwen Trust provides grants. Campaign with health professionals against vivisection.
- **Take care of animals.**
  Become a vet, stablehand, cattery assistant, RSPCA inspector, zoo keeper . . .

Animal Aid, The Old Chapel, Bradford Street, TONBRIDGE, Kent TN9 1AW. Tel: 01732 364546.

Big Cat Project: *see* **Born Free Foundation.**

Born Free Foundation (BFF), Coldharbour, DORKING, Surrey RH5 6HA. Tel: 01306 712091.

British Union for the Abolition of Vivisection (BUAV), 16A Crane Grove, LONDON N7 8LB. Tel: 0171 700 4888.

Catholic Study Circle for Animal Welfare, 39 Onslow Gardens, South Woodford, LONDON E18 1ND. Tel: 0181 989 0478.

Compassion in World Farming (CIWF), Charles House, 5a Charles Street, PETERSFIELD, Hampshire GU32 3EH. Tel: 01730 264208.

Doctors and Lawyers for Responsible Medicine, (DLRM): *see* **D – DISABILITY.**

Dr Hadwen Trust for Humane Research, 22 Bancroft, HITCHIN, Hertfordshire SG5 1JW. Tel: 01462 436819.

Elefriends: *see* **Born Free Foundation.**

Fellowship of Life, 43 Braichmelyn, Bethesda, BANGOR, Gwynedd LL57 3RD. Send a SAE for leaflets such as 'A Joyous Christmas for All Creation' and 'Calling all Christians and People of Goodwill'.

Friends of the Earth (FoE): *see* **E – ENVIRONMENT.**

Greenpeace: *see* **E – ENVIRONMENT.**

Humane Research Trust, Brook House, 29 Bramhall Lane South, Bramhall, STOCKPORT, Cheshire SK7 2DN. Tel: 0161 439 8041.

League Against Cruel Sports, Sparling House, 83–87 Union Street, LONDON SE1 1SG. Tel: 0171 403 6155.

Operation Wolf: *see* **Born Free Foundation.**

Orca Alert: *see* **Born Free Foundation.**

PETA (People for the Ethical Treatment of Animals), PO Box 3169, LONDON NW1 2JF. Tel: 0181 785 3113.

Quaker Concern for Animals, Angela Howard, Honorary Secretary, Webb's Cottage, Woolpits Road, Saling, BRAINTREE, Essex CM7 5DZ.

Royal Society for the Prevention of Cruelty to Animals (RSPCA), The Causeway, HORSHAM, West Sussex RH12 1HG. Tel: 01403 264181.

Royal Society for the Protection of Birds (RSPB): *see* **E – ENVIRONMENT.**

Shellfish Network, Box No. 66, c/o Greenleaf Bookshop, 82 Colston Street, BRISTOL BS1 5BB.

Vanishing Species Campaign: *see* **WWF UK.**

Vegetarian Society: *see* **B – BODY POLITICS.**

World Society for the Protection of Animals, 2 Langley Lane, LONDON SW8 1TJ. Tel: 0171 793 0540.

WWF UK (World Wide Fund for Nature): *see* **E – ENVIRONMENT.**

Zoo Check: *see* **Born Free Foundation.**

NOTES

INTRODUCTION

1 James 2.26.
2 Luke 10.25–37.

A – AIDS

1 'On the trail of the killer', *Guardian*, 1 December 1994, section 2, pp. 2–3.
2 Radlett, Marty. 'AIDS and children: a family disease', *Panos Mini Dossier*, no. 2, 1989, p. i.
3 Radlett, 'AIDS and children', p. i.
4 'AIDS and HIV-1 infection in the United Kingdom: monthly report', *Communicable Disease Report*, vol. 7, no. 4, 24 January 1997, p. 29.
5 'AIDS: five new cases every day', *Mildmay Annual Report*, 1994, p. 3.
6 Thompson, Tony, 'AIDS centres ignore elderly', *Time Out*, 3 July 1996, p. 11.
7 'Health news. Findings', *Vogue*, vol. 161, no. 2366, September 1995, p. 324.
8 Kauma, Bishop, Prayer, in *3rd Track*, Tear Fund, Issue 5.13.

C – CHILDREN

1 Foxen, Astrid, *Street Children*, Factsheet, Tear Fund, 1994.
2 Facts and figures, *Media Briefing on Toy Industry*, Press release, CIIR/TUC/WDM, 14 December 1995.
3 Child Poverty Action Group, *Key Poverty Statistics*, Leaflet, 1996, p. 1.
4 Davies, Nick, 'Please, sir, I want to be a prostitute', Stories from the Streets Series, *Guardian*, 29 August 1994.

D – DISABILITY

1 World Cancer Research Fund, Leaflet PFBWFL2, 1995.
2 Goldberg, Pamela, *This Year 25,000 Women . . .*, Mailing, Breast Cancer Campaign, 20 November 1995.

3   Timms, Nicholas, '"Social map" shows growing health and wealth divide', *The Independent*, 28 September 1995.

4   'The scandal of arthritis drugs', Leaflet, Plan 2000, 1995.

5   Usborne, David, 'Clinton faces life and death health battle', *The Independent on Sunday*, 14 August 1994, p. 14.

E – ENVIRONMENT

1   Kunru, Hari, 'Slag heaps in the sky', *Wired*, April 1996, p. 16.

2   Nicholson-Lord, David, 'How long have we got?', *The Independent on Sunday* (Sunday Review), 31 May 1992, p. 3.

3   *Corporate Giants*, World Development Movement, 1996.

4   *Leave Your Car at Home*, Leaflet, Friends of the Earth, 1995.

5   *Save Our Wild Places!*, Leaflet, Friends of the Earth, 1994.

6   *Lost: 95% of Flower-rich Meadows . . .*, Leaflet, RBR03, Council for the Preservation of Rural England.

7   Nicholson-Lord, 'How long have we got?'.

F – FEMINISM

1   *New Internationalist*, February 1993.

2   Greenburg, Susan *et al.*, 'Woman Power', *Newsweek* (Special Report), 9 March 1992, p. 28.

3   Postscript to the film *The Accused*.

4   Mullen, Lisa, 'Hail fellas, well Met', *Time Out* ('Time In' section), 26 June 1996, p. 177.

5   This, and all statistics without note numbers up to bullet eight, are taken from Parris, Kay, 'Still a world apart', *The Big Issue*, 4–10 September 1995, no. 146, p. 8.

6   Mills, Heather, 'Men "would use force in home"', *The Independent*, 18 January 1994.

G – GAMBLING

1   Barnett, Anthony, 'No-score draws', *Time Out*, 15–22 November 1995, pp. 12, 14.

H – HOMELESSNESS

1   Spackman, Anne, 'House or flat? Town or country? Big or small? Rent or buy?' *The Independent on Sunday*, 26 March 1995. p. 12.

2   Meikie, James, 'Increase in home repossessions', *Guardian*, 3 June 1996, p. 10.

3   *An Introduction to Crisis*, Leaflet, Crisis, 1995.

4 Rutman, Paul, 'Domestic violence: whose side is the law on?' *The Big Issue*, no. 157, 20–26 November, 1995, p. 8.
5 Age Concern figures, 1991.
6 Shelter figures, 1993.

I – INVESTMENT

1 National Opinion Poll survey on behalf of Friends Provident conducted by phone among sample of 1,000 adults structured to be representative of the British population, May 1995.
2 World Development Movement, *Corporate Giants: Their Grip on the World's Economy*, Briefing Paper, World Development Movement, 1996.
3 *Ethical Investment – What Is It?*, no. 1, Barchester Green Investment, p. 1.

M – MONEY

1 World Development Movement, *Corporate Giants: Their Grip on the World's Economy*, Briefing Paper, World Development Movement, 1996.
2 Donovan Patrick, 'Treasury bangs the drum for lost cause', *Guardian*, 19 August 1995, p. 33.

P – POVERTY

1 Key poverty statistics, Leaflet, Child Poverty Action Group, 1996.
2 Crisis, 1994.

R – RIGHTS

1 Ward, Rachel, Medical Foundation for the Care of the Victims of Torture mailing, Statement, 18 March 1996.
2 Survival International leaflet.
3 Lamb, Harriet, 'Aiding and abetting', *Spur*, World Development Movement, January 1996, p. 5.
4 *Who Speaks for Us?* Ramblers Association leaflet, 1990.
5 Neile, Euranis, 'Sick-birth caravans', *Nursing Standard*, 5 May 1993.

T – THIRD WORLD

1 Nutbrown, Ivan, 'Aid slash threat; opposition mounts', *Spur*, World Development Movement, November/December 1995, p. 1.
2 Tanner, John, 'Downward slide of poorest', *Spur*, World Development Movement, November/December 1995, p. 1.

3 Lamb, Harriet, *Worked to Death*, Campaign Mailing, World Development Movement, 1995.
4 United Nations Development Programme, *Human Development Report 1994*.
5 WDM, *Corporate Giants*, World Development Movement, 1995.
6 Holderness, Mike, 'Through the net', *Spur*, World Development Movement, January 1996, p. 4.

U – UNEMPLOYMENT

1 Bassett, Peter, 'Tackling the scourge of global unemployment', *The Times*, 31 January 1994.
2 Central Statistical Office, *Social Trends 27*, 1997.
3 'How to survive the 21st century', *The Independent on Sunday*, 26 March 1995, p. 6.

V – VIDEO VIOLENCE

1 Mills, Heather, 'Men "would use force in home"', *The Independent*, 18 January 1994.
2 Trower, Marcus, and Salisbury, Mark, 'A head doctor writes' . . . Interview with psychiatrist Dr Raj Persaud, *Empire* 1992 (EMAP Metro), p. 89.
3 Carey, Lavinia, 'Faulty figures', Letters, *Screen International*, 5 July 1996, p. 9.

W – WAR

1 Tear Fund, *Third World Facts*, Factsheet, June 1994.
2 United Nations Development Programme, *Human Development Report 1994*.

X – XENOPHOBIA

1 *Tales from the Wasteland*, Channel 4, Broke! Series, 6 June 1996.
2 Julian Kossoff, 'Camden in crime crisis', *Time Out*, 15 November 1995.

Y – YOUTH

1 Lepkowska, Dorothy, 'Heads blame violence on the failure of parents', *Evening Standard*, 22 September 1995.
2 Jury, Louise, 'Rave culture link brings greater risk in Britain', *The Independent*, 17 November 1995.
3 Davies, Nick, 'Please sir, I want to be a prostitute', *Guardian*, Stories from the Streets series, 29 August 1994.

4   Walden, George, 'Why we cannot let 14 year olds fall into an abyss', *London Evening Standard*, 26 September 1995.

Z – ZOOLOGY

1   Pellew, Dr Robin, *This Is the Biggest, Most Urgent Campaign WWF Has Ever Launched*, Leaflet, Worldwide Fund for Nature, October 1995.
2   *The End Is in Sight*, World Wide Fund for Nature, 1995, 95VSD2.
3   CIWF, *Sent Abroad to Suffer*, Leaflet, Compassion in World Farming, 1995.
4   Animal Aid, *Their Future Is in Your Hands*, Leaflet, Animal Aid, 1995.
5   The Fellowship of Life, *Newsletter*, Christmas 1995, p. 4.
6   *Doctors in Britain Against Animal Experiments*, Leaflet.

BIBLIOGRAPHY

(Where a price is given for a book or pamphlet, this was correct at the date of publication.)

A – AIDS

Chapman, Christine, *In Love Abiding* (Triangle/SPCK, 1995).

Dixon, Dr Patrick, *The Truth About AIDS* (Kingsway, 1994. 3rd edn).

Garfield, Simon, *The End of Innocence: Britain in the Time of AIDS* (Faber & Faber, 1994).

Goodrich, Joanna *et al.*, *Sexual Health*, Health Update no. 4. (HEA, 1994).

Hampton, Janie, *Meeting AIDS With Compassion*, Strategies for Hope Series no. 4. (Action Aid/AMREF/World in Need).

Health Education Authority, *HIV and AIDS: A Guide for Journalists* (HEA, 1993). 50p. Available from HEA, Hamilton House, Mabledon Place, London WC1H 9TX.

Mukoyogo, M. Christian, and Williams, Glen, *AIDS Orphans*, Strategies for Hope Series no. 5 (Action Aid/AMREF/World in Need).

Panos Institute, The, *Panos World-wide* (1989–). Available from the Panos Institute, 8 Alfred Place, London WC1E 7EB.

Richardson, Ann, and Bolle, Dietmar, *Wise Before Their Time* (Fount, 1992).

Smith, Trevor A., *AIDS Care* (Salvation Army). Available from Salvation Army, 105–109 Judd Street, London WC1H.

Ward, Hannah (ed.), *AIDS: A Challenge to the Churches* (BCC/FCFC, 1988). Available from BCC, Inter-Church House, 35–41 Lower Marsh, London SE1 7RL.

World Council of Churches, *A Guide to HIV/AIDS Pastoral Counselling* (WCC). Available from WCC, Unit 11, BP 2100, 1211 Geneva 2, Switzerland.

World Health Organization Global programme on AIDS, *The HIV/ AIDS Pandemic: 1994 Overview*, Ref: WHO/GPA/TCO/SEF/94.4 (World Health Organization, 1994).

B – BODY POLITICS

Bray-Garretson, Helen, and Cook, Kaye V., *Chaotic Eating* (Zondervan, 1992).

Classic Combinations, PO Box 123, Manchester M99 2BQ.

Conley, Rosemary, *Rosemary Conley's Complete Hip and Thigh Diet* (Arrow, 1989).

Filleul, Elizabeth, *Consuming Passion* (Triangle/SPCK, 1996).

Health Education Authority, *Guide to Healthy Eating*, Look After Your Heart Campaign (HEA, 1989). Free. Available from HEA, Hamilton House, Mabledon Place, London WC1H 9TX.

Lacey, Dr Richard, *Safe Shopping, Safe Cooking, Safe Eating* (Penguin, 1989).

Starkey, Mike, *Fashion and Style* (Monarch, 1995).

Tesco, *The Healthy Eating Guide for Children*, Leaflet (Tesco Stores Ltd, 1995).

von Ruhland, Catherine, *Glorious Food* (Marshall Pickering, 1992).

Wilkinson, Helena, *Beyond Chaotic Eating* (Marshall Pickering, 1993).

C – CHILDREN

Amnesty International, *Childhood Stolen: Grave Human Rights Abuses Against Children* (Amnesty International, 1995). £6.99. Available from Amnesty International, 99–119 Rosebery Avenue, London EC1R 4RE.

Department of Health, *Drugs and Solvents: A Young Person's Guide* (June 1994). Free. Available from BAPS, Health Publications Unit, DSS Distribution Centre, Heywood Stores, Manchester Road, Heywood, Lancs OL10 2PZ.

Holman, Bob, *Children and Crime* (Lion, 1995).

Jubilee Action, *Child Prostitution* (Jubilee Action, 1994). £7. Available from Jubilee Action, St John's, Cranleigh Road, Wonersh, Guildford GU5 OQX.

Mette, Norbert, and Junker-Kenny, Maureen (eds), *Little Children Suffer* (SCM, 1996).

TACADE, *Drugs and Solvents; You and Your Child* (Department of Health, Ref DYYC, March 1994). Free. Available from BAPS, Health Publications Unit, DSS Distribution Centre, Heywood Stores, Manchester Road, Heywood, Lancs OL10 2PZ.

UNICEF, *State of the World's Children*, Annual (UNICEF).

Arnold, Peter *et al.*, *Community Care: The Housing Dimension* (Joseph Rowntree Foundation, 1994). £6.50. Available from York Publishing Services Ltd, 64 Hallfield Road, Layerthorpe, York YO3 7XQ.

Baldock, John, and Ungerson, Claire, *Becoming Consumers of Community Care: Households within the Mixed Economy of Welfare* (Joseph Rowntree Foundation, 1994). £8.50. Available from York Publishing Services Ltd, 64 Hallfield Road, Layerthorpe, York YO3 7XQ.

Baum, Michael, and Denton, Sylvie, *Breast Cancer: The Facts* (Oxford University Press, 1988, 2nd edn).

Beresford, Bryony, *Expert Opinions: A National Survey of Parents Caring for a Severely Disabled Child* (Policy Press, 1995). £10.50. Available from York Publishing Services Ltd, 64 Hallfield Road, Layerthorpe, York YO3 7XQ.

Bewley, Catherine, and Glendinning, Caroline, *Involving Disabled People in Community Care Planning* (Joseph Rowntree Foundation, 1994). £8.50. Available from York Publishing Services Ltd, 64 Hallfield Road, Layerthorpe, York YO3 7XQ.

Brady, Joan, *Death Comes for Peter Pan* (Secker & Warburg, 1996).

Chapman, Christine, *In Love Abiding* (Triangle/SPCK, 1995).

Ciba Laboratories, *Breast Awareness; Information for Patients* (Ciba-Geigy Plc, May 1995). Free. Available from your GP or the Women's Nationwide Cancer Control Campaign, Sauna House, 128/130 Curtain Road, London EC2A 3AR.

Goss, Sue, and Miller, Clive, *From Margin to Mainstream: Developing User and Carer-centred Community Care* (Joseph Rowntree Foundation, 1995). £9. Available from York Publishing Services Ltd, 64 Hallfield Road, Layerthorpe, York YO3 7XQ.

Lovelock, Robin *et al*,. *Shared Territory: Assessing the Social Support Needs of Visually Impaired People* (Joseph Rowntree Foundation, 1995. £9. Available from York Publishing Services Ltd, 64 Hallfield Road, Layerthorpe, York YO3 7XQ.

Maddocks, Morris, *The Christian Healing Ministry* (SPCK, 1995, 3rd edn).

McMillen, S. I., *None of These Diseases* (Marshall Pickering, 1984, 2nd edn).

Millwood, Alan, and Skidmore, David, *Local Authority Management of Special Needs* (YPS, 1995). £8.50. Available from York Publishing Services Ltd, 64 Hallfield Road, Layerthorpe, York YO3 7XQ.

Thornton, Patricia, and Mountain, Gail, *A Positive Response: Developing Community Alarm Services for Older People* (Joseph Rowntree Foundation, 1992). £6.50. Available from York Publishing Services Ltd, 64 Hallfield Road, Layerthorpe, York YO3 7XQ.

Thornton, Patricia, and Tozer, Rosemary, *Having a Say in Change: Older People and Community Care* (Joseph Rowntree Foundation, 1995). £8.50. Available from York Publishing Services Ltd, 64 Hallfield Road, Layerthorpe, York YO3 7XQ.

World Cancer Research Fund, *Dietary Guidelines to Lower Your Cancer Risk* (World Cancer Research Fund). Free. Available from World Cancer Research Fund, 11/12 Buckingham Gate, London SW1E 6LB.

E – ENVIRONMENT

CAFOD, *Renewing the Earth* (CAFOD, 1989). £2.50. Available from CAFOD, 2 Romero Close, Stockwell Road, London SW9 9TY.

Christian Ecology Link, *Steps Towards Sustainability* (CEL, 1994). £4. Available from CEL, 20 Carlton Road, Harrogate, North Yorkshire HG2 8DD.

Cooper, Tim, *Green Christianity* (Spire, 1990).

Elkington, John, and Hailes, Julia, *The Green Consumer Guide* (Victor Gollancz, 1989).

Elsdon, Ron, *Greenhouse Theology* (Monarch, 1992).

Environment Department, *Environmental Bulletin*, Quarterly (World Bank). Details from the World Bank, 1818 H Street, NW Washington DC 20433, USA.

Environment Department, *The World Bank and the Environment*, Annual (World Bank, 1990–).

Friends of the Earth, *Cars Cost the Earth* (FoE, 1995). 50p. Available from FoE Publications Despatch, 56–58 Alma Street, Luton LU1 2YZ.

Friends of the Earth, *Gaining interest* (FoE, 1994). £6. Available from FoE Publications Despatch, 56–58 Alma Street, Luton LU1 2YZ.

Friends of the Earth, *Planet Savers* (FoE, May 1995). Free. Available from FoE Publications Despatch, 56–58 Alma Street, Luton LU1 2YZ.

Hall, Jeremy, *Real Lives, Half Lives* (Penguin, 1996).

Lean, Geoffrey, and Hinrichson, Jan, *Atlas of the Environment* (Helicon, 1992).

Milner, J. Edward, Filby, Carol, and Board, Marian, *The Green Index* (Cassell, 1990).

Myers, Norman (ed.), *The Gaia Atlas of Planet Management* (Pan, 1985).

Porritt, Jonathon, *Seeing Green* (Basil Blackwell, 1984).

Rifkin, Jeremy, *Biosphere Politics* (HarperCollins Religious, 1992).

Shoard, Marion, *This Land Is Our Land* (Paladin, 1987).

Taylor, John V., *Enough Is Enough* (SCM, 1975).

Tear Fund, 'Whose earth?' *Third Track*, issue 11, April 1992. Available from Tear Fund, 100 Church Road, Teddington, Middlesex TW11 8QE.

von Ruhland, Catherine, *Going Green* (Marshall Pickering, 1992).

Webb, Mike (ed.), *The Earth Is the Lord's*, Tear Fund Profile Booklet (Tear Fund). 75p. Available from Tear Fund, 100 Church Road, Teddington, Middlesex TW11 8QE.

Williams, Heathcote, *Autogeddon* (Jonathan Cape, 1991).

World Bank, *World Development Report 1992: Development and the Environment* (World Bank, 1992).

World Wide Fund for Nature, *Gardening for Wildlife: Litter to Leaf* (WWF, 1994). Available from WWF(UK), Panda House, Weyside Park, Godalming, Surrey GU7 1XR.

World Wide Fund for Nature, *The Greenhouse Effect: What You Should Know* (WWF, 1991). Available from WWF(UK), Panda House, Weyside Park, Godalming, Surrey GU7 1XR.

F – FEMINISM

Amnesty International, *Human Rights Are Women's Rights* (Amnesty International, 1995). £6.99. Available from Amnesty International, 99–119 Rosebery Avenue, London EC1R 4RE.

Fischer, Kathleen, *Autumn Gospel* (SPCK, 1996).

Furlong, Monica, and the St Hilda Community, *Women Included* (SPCK, 1996, 2nd edn).

Greer, Germaine, *The Female Eunuch* (Macgibbon, 1970).

Hampson, Daphne, *Swallowing a Fishbone* (SPCK, 1996).

Joshi, Heather *et al.*, *Dependence and Independence in the Finances of Women Aged 33* (Family Policy Studies Centre, 1995). £9.50. Available from York Publishing Services Ltd, 64 Hallfield Road, Layerthorpe, York YO3 7XQ.

London Borough of Islington, *The Hidden Figure: Domestic Violence in North London* (1994). £8. Available from London Borough of Islington, Town Hall, Upper Street, London N1 2UD.

New Internationalist, *Women: A World Report* (Methuen/New Internationalist, 1985).

Oakley, Ann, *Housewife* (Penguin, 1976).

Peberdy, Alison (ed.), *Women Priests?*, Women and Religion Series edited by Janet Martin Soskice (Marshall Pickering, 1988).

Storkey, Elaine, *What's Right With Feminism* (SPCK, 1997, revised edn).

Wakeman, Hilary (ed.), *Women Priests: The First Years* (DLT, 1996).

G – GAMBLING

Camelot, *Fun for You. Funds for Projects Like These* (Camelot, 1995). Free. Available from National Lottery outlets.

Eastman, Dick, *Seven Keys to a Better Life* (Chosen, 1991).

Fitzherbert, Luke, *Winners and Losers: The Impact of the National Lottery* (YPS, 1995). £8.50. Available from York Publishing Services Ltd, 64 Hallfield Road, Layerthorpe, York YO3 7XQ.

Tondeur, Keith, *What Price the Lottery?* (Monarch, 1996).

H – HOMELESSNESS

Allen, Christine, *A Woman's Place: Reflection on Women's Housing Needs* (CHAS,1995). £6.95. Available from CHAS, 209 Old Marylebone Road, London NW1 5QT.

Bird, John (ed.), *The Big Issue* (1991–). Weekly; available from street vendors in UK cities.

Church Housing Aid Society, *For the Sake of Justice* (CHAS, 1995). Available from CHAS, 209 Old Marylebone Road, London NW1 5QT.

Goss, Sue, and Kent, Chris, *Health and Housing: Working Together?* (Policy Press, 1995). £11.50. Available from York Publishing Services Ltd, 64 Hallfield Road, Layerthorpe, York YO3 7XQ.

Handbook of London Services for Homeless People. Tel: 0181 600 3000 to order copies.

HMSO, *Our Future Homes* (HMSO, 1995). £8. Available from HMSO, PO Box 276, London SW8 5DT.

Murdoch, Alison, *In From The Cold* (Crisis, 1993). £4.00. Available from Crisis, 1st floor, Challenger House, 42 Adler Street, London E1 1EN.

St Mungo Association, *Inreach* (St Mungo Association/Esso, 1995).

Randall, Geoffrey, and Brown, Susan, *The Move in Experience* (Crisis, 1994). £6.95. Available from Crisis, 1st floor, Challenger House, 42 Adler Street, London E1 1EN.

Trench, Sally, *Bury Me in My Boots* (Hodder & Stoughton, 1968).

Turnham Elvins, Mark, *The Church's Response to the Homeless* (Mayhew McCrimmon, 1985).

UNLEASH, *Standing Alongside Homeless People* (UNLEASH). £5.00 inc. p & p. Available from UNLEASH, Trinity House, 4 Chapel Court, Borough High Street, London SE1 1HW.

YMCA, *Surviving the Cold* (YMCA). Free. Contact YMCA, 640 Forest Road, London E17 3DZ for copies to distribute to homeless people.

I – INVESTMENT

Childs Jnr, James M., *Ethics in Business* (Fortress Press, 1995).

Christian Ethical Investment Group, *Our Best Interest* (CEIG, 1994). £6. Available from CEIG, 90 Booker Avenue, Bradwell Common, Milton Keynes MK13 8EF.

'Harries (Bishop of Oxford) v. Church Commissioners', Times Law Report, *The Times*, 30 October 1991.

Holden Meehan, *The Independent Guide to Ethical and Green Investment Funds*, Annual (Holden Meehan). Call 0117 9252874 for a free copy.

Pearce, John, *At the Heart of the Community Economy* (Calouste Gulbenkian Foundation, 1995).

Schumacher, E. F., *Small Is Beautiful* (Abacus, 1974).

Zadek, Simon, and Evans, Richard, *Auditing the Market* (Traidcraft Exchange/New Economics, 1993). £2.50. Available from New Economics Foundation, Universal House, Second floor, 88–94 Wentworth Street, London E1 7SA.

'Can you invest ethically?', *Which? Magazine*, July 1993, pp. 46–9.

J – JUSTICE

Barraz, Oliver *et al.*, *Local Leadership and Decision-making: A Study of France, Germany, the United States and Britain* (LGC Communications, 1994). £8.50. Available from York Publishing Services Ltd, 64 Hallfield Road, Layerthorpe, York YO3 7XQ.

Crowe, Philip, *A Whisper Will Be Heard* (Fount, 1994).

Loughlin, Martin, *Administrative Accountability in Local Government* (Joseph Rowntree Foundation, 1993). £5.50. Available from York Publishing Services Ltd, 64 Hallfield Road, Layerthorpe, York YO3 7XQ.

Plummer, John, *The Governance Gap: Quangos and Accountability* (LCC Communications, 1994). £8.50. Available from York Publishing Services Ltd, 64 Hallfield Road, Layerthorpe, York YO3 7XQ.

K – KINGDOM

Allen, Durston *et al.*, *Sunday Monday* (Scripture Union/Cassell, 1995).

Brownfoot, Jan, and Wilks, Francis, *The Directory of Volunteer and Employment Opportunities* (Brownfoot and Wilks, 1993).

Clark, David M., *Good Neighbours: A Practical Guide to Setting Up a Village Care Group* (Joseph Rowntree Foundation, 1992). £5. Available from York Publishing Services Ltd, 64 Hallfield Road, Layerthorpe, York YO3 7XQ.

Fogerty, Michael, and Legard, Robin, *More than Money: How Businesses and Voluntary Organisations Can Work Together* (Joseph Rowntree Foundation, 1993). £5. Available from York Publishing Services Ltd, 64 Hallfield Road, Layerthorpe, York YO3 7XQ.

Hambleton, Robin *et al.*, *The Collaborative Council: A Study of Inter-agency Working in Practice* (LGC Communications, 1995). £11.50.

Holy Trinity Brompton, *Lifelines London* (Holy Trinity Brompton, 1995). Available from Holy Trinity Brompton, Brompton Road, London SW7 1JA.

Johnstone, Patrick, *Operation World* (OM/WEC Publishing, 1995, 5th edn).

NIV Study Bible (Hodder & Stoughton, 1987).

Sine, Tom, *The Mustard Seed Conspiracy* (Monarch, 1985).

L – LETTERS

Amnesty International, *A Brief Guide to Writing Letters* (Amnesty International). Free. Available from Amnesty International, 99–119 Rosebery Avenue, London EC1R 4RE.

Amnesty International, *Letter Writing Guide* (Amnesty International). £2.25. Available from Amnesty International, 99–119 Rosebery Avenue, London EC1R 4RE.

Prejean, Helen, *Dead Men Walking: An Experience of Death Row* (Fount, 1994).

M – MONEY

Central Board of Finance of the Church of England, *The Christian Stewardship of Money* (Central Board of Finance of the Church of England, 1970).

Evangelical Alliance and Credit Action, *Escape from Debt* (EA/Credit Action, 1993). £2.50. Available from EA, Whitefield House, 186 Kennington Park Road, London SE11 4BT.

Office of Fair Trading, *Moneyfax 4* (HMSO/Radio 1, 1995). Free.
Phone Radio 1 Line 0800 110 100 for a copy.
Webley, Simon, *Money Matters* (IVP, 1978).

N – NEGATIVES

Camus, Albert, *The Outsider* (Hamish Hamilton, 1984).
Cotterell, Peter, *Is God Helpless?* (Triangle/SPCK, 1996).
King, Peter, *Dark Night Spirituality* (SPCK, 1995).
Mother Teresa, *A Simple Path* (Random House, 1995).

O – ORGANIZATIONS

Handy, Charles, *The Age of Unreason* (Arrow, 1991, 2nd edn).
Hebblethwaite, Margaret, *Basic Is Beautiful* (Fount, 1993).
Pugh, D. S. (ed.), *Organisation Theory*, Modern Management Readings
(Penguin, 1971).

P – POVERTY

Alton, David, *Faith in Britain* (Hodder & Stoughton, 1991).
Barclay, Sir Peter, Chair, *Joseph Rowntree Foundation Inquiry into
Income and Wealth*, Vol. 1 (Joseph Rowntree Foundation, 1995).
£9. Available from York Publishing Services Ltd, 64 Hallfield Road,
Layerthorpe, York YO3 7XQ.
Bradshaw, Jonathon, *Household Budget and Living Standards* (Joseph
Rowntree Foundation, 1993). £7.50. Available from York
Publishing Services Ltd, 64 Hallfield Road, Layerthorpe, York YO3
7XQ.
Child Poverty Action Group, *Key Poverty Statistics*, Leaflet (Child
Poverty Action Group, 1996). Available from Child Poverty Action
Group, 4th floor, 1–5 Bath Street, London EC17 9PY.
Church of England, *Faith in the City* (Church House, 1985).
Dobson, B. *et al.*, *Diet, Choice and Poverty* (Family Policy Studies
Centre, 1994). £7.50. Available from York Publishing Services Ltd,
64 Hallfield Road, Layerthorpe, York YO3 7XQ.
Forrest, Ray, and Gordon, Dave, *People and Places* (School for
Advanced Urban Studies, 1993).
Goodman, Alison, and Webb, Steven, *For Richer and Poorer: The
Changing Distribution of Income in the UK, 1961–91* (Institute for
Fiscal Studies, 1994).
Hanson, Ingrid, *UK Action* (Tear Fund, 1996). 95p. Available from
Enquiry Unit, Tear Fund, 100 Church Road, Teddington,
Middlesex TW11 8QE.

Hills, John, and LSE Welfare State Programme, *The Future of Welfare* (Joseph Rowntree Foundation, 1993). £8.50. Available from York Publishing Services Ltd, 64 Hallfield Road, Layerthorpe, York YO3 7XQ.

HMSO, *Households Below Average Income: A Statistical Analysis 1979–1992/3* (October 1995, revised edn).

Joseph Rowntree Foundation, *Publications List*, November 1995–. Free. Contact York Publishing Services Ltd 64 Hallfield Road, Layerthorpe, York YO3 7XQ.

Mills, John, *Joseph Rowntree Foundation Inquiry into Income and Wealth*, Vol. 2 (Joseph Rowntree Foundation, 1995). £9/£15 for both vols.

Paget-Wilkes, Michael, *Poverty, Revolution and the Church* (Paternoster, 1991).

Russell, Hilary, *Poverty Close to Home* (Mowbray, 1995).

Sheppard, David, *Bias to the Poor* (Hodder & Stoughton, 1983).

Taylor, Marilyn, *Unleashing the Potential: Bringing Residents to the Centre of Regeneration* (Joseph Rowntree Foundation, 1995). Report, £10.50/Report & Video, £19. Available from York Publishing Services Ltd, 64 Hallfield Road, Layerthorpe, York YO3 7XQ.

Taylor, Michael, *Not Angels, but Agencies* (SCM, 1995).

Thake, Stephen, *Staying the Course: The Role and Structures of Community Regeneration Organisations* (YPS, 1995). £11.

Q – QUESTIONS

Blakely, C. M. (ed.), *Westminster Watch* (Evangelical Alliance/Church of England Newspaper). Available from Westminster Watch, 10 Little College Street, London SW1P 3SH. Westminster Watch Information Service: 0171 582 0228.

Mother Teresa, *A Simple Path* (Random House, 1995).

Peck, M. Scott., *A Different Drum* (Ulverscroft, 1987).

Rao, Nirmala, *Managing Change: Councillors and the New Local Government* (Joseph Rowntree Foundation, 1993). £5.50. Available from York Publishing Services Ltd, 64 Hallfield Road, Layerthorpe, York YO3 7XQ.

Stott, John, *Issues Facing Christians Today* (Hodder & Stoughton, revised edn).

Tomlinson, Dave, *The Post-evangelical* (Triangle/SPCK, 1995).

Walsh, Brian, and Middleton, Richard, *Truth Is Stranger Than It Used To Be*, Gospel and Culture, (SPCK, 1995).

Young, Roger W, *Everybody's Business* (Oxford University Press, 1968).

R – RIGHTS

Amnesty International, *The Amnesty International Report*, Annual (Amnesty International).

Amnesty International, *Books Catalogue*, Annual (Amnesty International). Free. Available from Amnesty International, 99–119 Rosebery Avenue, London EC1R 4RE.

Amnesty International, *Getting Away with Murder* (Amnesty International, 1993). £5.99. Available from Amnesty International, 99–119 Rosebery Avenue, London EC1R 4RE.

Amnesty International, *Political Killings and 'Disappearances'* (Amnesty International, 1994). £9.99. Available from Amnesty International, 99–119 Rosebery Avenue, London EC1R 4RE.

Amnesty International, *Prisoners Without a Voice* (Amnesty International, 1994). £6.99. Available from Amnesty International, 99–119 Rosebery Avenue, London EC1R 4RE.

Amnesty International, *When the State Kills: The Death Penalty v. Human Rights* (Amnesty International, 1989). £9.99. Available from Amnesty International, 99–119 Rosebery Avenue, London EC1R 4RE.

Bronson, Marsha, *Organisations that Help the World: Amnesty International* (Exley, 1993).

Shaw, Sue (ed.), *New Internationalist*, no. 229 (March 1992).

United Nations, *Universal Declaration of Human Rights* (United Nations, 1948). Available from Amnesty International, 99–119 Rosebery Avenue, London EC1R 4RE.

Wright, Christopher, *Human Rights: A Study in Biblical Themes*, Grove Booklet on Ethics no. 31 (Grove Books).

Wright, Christopher, *Human Rights*, Bible Study Booklet no. 3 (Tear Fund).

S – SOCIETY

CARE, *Action File*, Briefing Series (Care, 1995–). £10. Available from Luke Whitcomb, CARE, Freepost WD1079, London SW1P 3YZ.

Christians for Social Justice, *Christian Responsibility in the World* (CSJ, 1996). £5. Available from CSJ, 31 Prince of Wales Lane, Yardley Wood, Birmingham B14 4LB.

Christian Service Centre, *STS Directory*, Annual (Christian Service

Centre). £4.75. Available from SCS, Holloway Street West, Lower Gornal, Dudley, West Midlands DY3 2DZ.

Comby, Jean, *How to Understand Christian Mission* (SCM, 1996).

Sider, Ronald, *Bread of Life* (Triangle/SPCK, 1996).

Thomas, Norman, *Readings in World Mission* (SPCK, 1995).

Brierley, Peter, and Wraight, Heather (eds), *UK Christian Handbook*, Annual (Christian Research).

Wolfe, John, *Evangelical Faith and Public Zeal* (SPCK, 1995).

T – THIRD WORLD

Boff, Leonardo, and Pieris, Aloysius (eds), *Ecology and Poverty* (SCM, 1995).

Christian Aid, *Trade for Change* (Christian Aid). Free. Available from Christian Aid, PO Box 100, London SE1 7RT.

Christian Aid, *Who Runs the World?* (Christian Aid). Free. Available from Christian Aid, PO Box 100, London SE1 7RT.

George, Susan, *How the Other Half Dies* (Penguin, 1986).

Jackson, Ben, *Poverty and the Planet* (WDM/Penguin, 1990).

Keay, Kathy, *How to Make the World Less Hungry* (Frameworks, 1990).

Oxfam/Christian Aid, *Making Money* (Oxfam/Christian Aid, 1984). Free. Available from Oxfam, 274 Banbury Road, Oxford OX2 7DZ or Christian Aid, PO Box 100, London SE1 7RT.

Reed, Andrew, *The Developing World* (Unwin Hyman, 1987, 2nd edn).

Sampson, Anthony, *North–South: A Programme for Survival*, The Report of the Independent Commission on International Development Issues under the chairmanship of Willy Brandt, World Affairs Series (Pan, 1980).

Sider, Ronald, *Rich Christians in an Age of Hunger* (Hodder & Stoughton, 1978).

Simon, Arthur, *Bread for the World* (Eerdmanns, 1984, revised edn).

Stubbs, Lucy (ed.), *The Third World Directory*, Annual (Directory of Social Change). £9.95. Available from Directory of Social Change, Radius Works, Back Lane, London NW3 1HL.

Tear Fund, *A Gift of Hope*, Leaflet (Tear Fund). Free. Available from Tear Fund, 100 Church Road, Teddington, Middlesex TW11 8QE.

Tear Fund, *Resources* (Annual). Free. Available from Tear Fund, 100 Church Road, Teddington, Middlesex TW11 8QE.

Tear Fund, *Tear Fund TV* (Resource Pack, 1995). £12 + £1 p & p. Available from Tear Fund, 100 Church Road, Teddington, Middlesex TW11 8QE.

Tear Fund Communications Department, *Third World Facts*, Information Sheet (Tear Fund). Available from Tear Fund, 100 Church Road, Teddington, Middlesex TW11 8QE.

WDM, *British Overseas Aid – Spending Trends*, Briefing (WDM, 1996). £1.75. Available from WDM, 25 Beehive Place, London SW9 7QR.

WDM, *Corporate Giants: Their Grip on the World Economy*, Briefing PR466 (WDM, 1996). 50p. Available from WDM, 25 Beehive Place, London SW9 7QR.

WDM, *Fight World Poverty Lobby* (WDM, 1985). Available from WDM, 25 Beehive Place, London SW9 7QR.

WDM, *Publications List and Order Form*, Leaflet (WDM, 1995). Free. Available from WDM, 25 Beehive Place, London SW9 7QR.

WDM, *Trade* (WDM, October 1993). Available from WDM, 25 Beehive Place, London SW9 7QR.

Wells, Phil, and Jetter, Mandy, *The Global Consumer* (Gollancz, 1991).

Wilkinson, Anne, *It's Not Fair!* (Christian Aid, 1985). £2. Available from Christian Aid, PO Box No 1, London SW9 8BH.

Worldaware, *Worldaware Resources Catalogue*, Annual (Worldaware). Available from Worldaware, 2 Cotton Street, London WC1R 4AB.

World Bank, *World Development Report*, Annual (World Bank). Contact World Bank, 1818 H Street, NW Washington DC 20433, USA, for details.

World Bank, *World Development Report 1992: Development and the Environment* (World Bank, 1992). Contact World Bank, 1818 H Street, NW Washington DC 20433, USA, for details.

Wynne-Tyson, Jon, *Food for a Future* (Thorsons, 1988, revised edn).

U – UNEMPLOYMENT

(See also **P – POVERTY.**)

Christians Abroad, *World Service Enquiry* (1996 Guide).

Orwell, George, *The Road to Wigan Pier* (Secker & Warburg, 1959).

V – VIDEO VIOLENCE

BVA, *Mum, Can I Watch a Video?* (BVA, 1995). Free. Available from your video dealer or the BVA, 22 Poland Street, London W1V 3DD.

ELSPA, *A Parent's Guide to Computer and Video Games* (ELSPA, 1995). Free. From games dealers or ELSPA, Station Road, Offenham, Evesham, Worcester WR11 5LW.

French, Karl (ed.), *Screen Violence* (Bloomsbury, 1996).

Medved, Michael, *Hollywood Versus America* (HarperCollins, 1992).

W – WAR

Brittain, Vera, *Testament of Youth* (Gollancz, 1978).

de la Billiere, Sir Peter, *Storm Command* (HarperCollins, 1992).

Frank, Anne, *The Diary of Anne Frank* (Pan, 1989).

Glynn, Paul, *A Song for Nagasaki* (Fount, 1988).

Grossman, David, *See Under: Love* (Cape, 1990).

Keneally, Thomas, *Schindler's List* (Sceptre, 1986).

Lee, Laurie, *As I Walked Out One Midsummer Morning* (André Deutsch, 1969).

Ninh, Bao, *The Sorrow of War* (Secker & Warburg, 1993).

WDM, *Gunrunners Gold: How the Public's Money Finances Arms Sales* (WDM, 1995). £4.50. Available from WDM, 25 Beehive Place, London SW9 7QR.

WDM, *Nigeria – The Case for an Arms Embargo*, Briefing (WDM, 1995). Free. Available from WDM, 25 Beehive Place, London SW9 7QR.

Wollaston, Isabel, *A War Against Memory?* (SPCK, 1996).

X – XENOPHOBIA

Baldwin, James, 'Nobody knows my name', in Young, Roger W., *Everybody's Business* (Oxford University Press, 1968).

Bowen, Roger, *So I Send You*, International Study Guide Series 34 (SPCK, 1996).

Catholic Association for Racial Justice, *Racism in British Society* (CARJ, 1994).

Christians Aware, *Refugees – Seeing the Whole Picture?* (Christians Aware). Free. Available from Christians Aware, 10 Springfield Road, Leicester LE2 3BD.

Paldiel, Mordecai, *Sheltering the Jews* (Fortress Press, 1995).

Refugee Council, *Appeal for Emergency Provision for Asylum Seekers*, Briefing (Refugee Council, December 1995). Available from Refugee Council, 3 Bondway, London SW8 1SJ.

Society of Friends, *Quakers and Race*, Biannual, Community & Care Committee, QSRE.

Society of Friends, *Worship without Prejudice* (Friends House, 1992). Further information from Friends House, Euston Road, London NW1 2BJ.

UNHCR, *Refugees*, Quarterly. Public Information Service of the United Nations High Commissioner for Refugees. Free. Available from UNHCR, PO Box 2500, 1211 Geneva 2 Depot, Switzerland.

UNHCR, *The State of the World's Refugees*, Annual (UNHCR). Details from UNHCR, PO Box 2500, 1211 Geneva 2 Depot, Switzerland.

Y – YOUTH

Central Office of Information, *Drug and Solvent Abuse* (Department of Health, December 1993). Free. Available from BAPS, Health Publications Unit, DSS Distribution Centre, Heywood Stores, Manchester Road, Heywood, Lancashire OL10 2PZ.

Central Office of Information, *Drugs and Solvents: Things You Should Know* (Department of Health, March 1994). For 13–18-year-olds. Free. Available from BAPS, Health Publications Unit, DSS Distribution Centre, Heywood Stores, Manchester Road, Heywood, Lancashire OL10 2PZ.

Demos, *Freedom's Children* (Demos, 1995).

Fast-moving Currents in Youth Culture (Lynx, 1995).

Herbert, Martin, *Living With Teenagers* (Basil Blackwell, 1987).

Open University, *Parents and Teenagers*. Study Pack. Open University. £25. Available from Open University Learning Materials Service, Milton Keynes MK7 6DH.

TACADE, *Drugs and Solvents; You and Your Child*, Department of Health, Ref DYYC (March 1994). Free. Available from BAPS, Health Publications Unit, DSS Distribution Centre, Heywood Stores, Manchester Road, Heywood, Lancs OL10 2PZ.

Ward, Pete, *Worship and Youth Culture* (Marshall Pickering, 1993).

Ward, Pete, *Youth Culture and the Gospel* (Marshall Pickering, 1992).

Z – ZOOLOGY

Animal Aid, *Recipe for Life* (Animal Aid, 1996). Free. Available from Animal Aid, The Old Chapel, Bradford Street, Tonbridge, Kent TN9 1AW.

Baker, Bishop Dr John Austin, *Is the Tide Turning?*, Address to the AGM of the Catholic Study Circle for Animal Welfare, 19 October 1994 (CSCAW, 1994). Available from CSCAW, 39 Onslow Gardens, South Woodford, London E18 1ND.

Bowler, Jane, *The Vegetarian Handbook* (The Vegetarian Society of the UK, 1990).

BUAV, *Approved Product Guide*, Annual (British Union for the Abolition of Vivisection). Free. Available from BUAV, 16a Crane Grove, London N7 8LB.

Catholic Study Circle for Animal Welfare, *The Ark*, Quarterly (1937–).

Available from CSCAW, 39 Onslow Gardens, South Woodford, London E18 1ND.

Clements, Kath, *Why Vegan?* (GMP, 1985).

Croce, Professor Pietro, *Vivisection or Science?* (Doctors and Lawyers for Responsible Medicine). £9. Available from DLRM, 104B Weston Park, London N8 9PP.

Eaton, John, *The Circle of Creation* (SCM, 1995).

Lacey, Professor Richard, *Mad Cow Disease* (Cypsela, 1994).

Linzey, Andrew, *Animal Theology* (SCM, 1994).

RSPCA, *A Horse of Your Own*, Leaflet (RSPCA). Free. Available from RSPCA, The Causeway, Horsham, West Sussex RH12 1HG.

Scott, Shirley and Michael, *A Little Book of Vegetarian Recipes* (M. G. Scott, 1986). 90p. Available from M. G. Scott, Blo' Norton Hall, near Diss, Norfolk 1P22 2JD.

Singer, Peter, *Animal Liberation* (Pimlico, 1995, 2nd edn).

Williams, Heathcote, *Whale Nation* (Jonathan Cape, 1988).

World Council of Churches, *Liberation of Life*. Report from the Churchand Society Consultation of the World Council of Churches, Geneva, meeting at Amnecy, France, September 1988. Available from WCC, PO Box 2100, CH–1211 Geneva 2, Switzerland.

World Society for the Protection of Animals and Born Free Foundation, *The Zoo Inquiry* (WSPA/BFF, 1994). £9.50. Available from BFF, Coldharbour, Dorking, Surrey RH5 6HA.

168

POSTSCRIPT

When the song of the angels is still,

When the star in the sky is gone,

When the kings and princes are home,

When the shepherds are back with their sheep,

The work of Christmas begins:

To find the lost

To heal the broken

To feed the hungry

To release the prisoners

To rebuild the nations

To bring peace among people

To make music in the heart.

Author unknown

SPCK

The Society for Promoting Christian Knowledge (SPCK) has as its purpose three main tasks:

- **Communicating the Christian faith in its rich diversity**

- **Helping people to understand the Christian faith and to develop their personal faith**

- **Equipping Christians for mission and ministry**

SPCK Worldwide serves the Church through Christian literature and communication projects in over 100 countries. Special schemes also provide books for those training for ministry in many parts of the developing world. SPCK Worldwide's ministry involves Churches of many traditions. This worldwide service depends upon the generosity of others and all gifts are spent wholly on ministry programmes, without deductions.

SPCK Bookshops support the life of the Christian community by making available a full range of Christian literature and other resources, and by providing support to bookstalls and book agents throughout the UK. SPCK Bookshops' mail order department meets the needs of overseas customers and those unable to have access to local bookshops.

SPCK Publishing produces Christian books and resources, covering a wide range of inspirational, pastoral, practical and academic subjects. Authors are drawn from many different Christian traditions, and publications aim to meet the needs of a wide variety of readers in the UK and throughout the world.

The Society does not necessarily endorse the individual views contained in its publications, but hopes they stimulate readers to think about and further develop their Christian faith.

For further information about the Society, please write to: SPCK, Holy Trinity Church, Marylebone Road, London NW1 4DU, United Kingdom. Telephone: 0171 387 5282